OUR LIFE IS LOVE:

The Quaker Spiritual Journey

Marcelle Martin

Inner Light Books
San Francisco, California
2016

D1286541

Our Life Is Love: The Quaker Spiritual Journey
© 2016 by Marcelle Martin

Grateful acknowledgment is made for permission to reprint from copyrighted material: To Quakers Uniting in Publications and Quaker Press to quote from *Spirit Rising: Young Quaker Voices* © 2010, Conti et al., eds. To Friends United Press to quote from *Walk Worthy of Your Calling* © 2004, Margery Post Abbott and Peggy Senger Parsons, eds.; *Growing Up Plain: The Journey of a Public Friend* © 1999, Wilmer A. Cooper; and *Inner Tenderings* ©1996, Louise Wilson. Permissions continue on page 195, which constitutes a continuation of this copyright page.

Cover and book design: Charles Martin

Published by Inner Light Books, San Francisco, California
www.innerlightbooks.com
editor@innerlightbooks.com

Library of Congress Control Number: 2015958959

ISBN 978–0-9970604–0-9 (hardcover)
ISBN 978–0-9970604–1-6(paperback)
ISBN 978–0-9970604–2-5 (eBook)

Our life is love, and peace, and tenderness; and bearing one with another, and forgiving one another, and not laying accusations one against another; but praying one for another, and helping one another up with a tender hand. . . . So mind Truth . . . [and] be a good savor in the places where ye live, the meek, innocent, tender, righteous life reigning in you, governing over you, and shining through you, in the eyes of all with whom ye converse.

—Isaac Penington, 1667

Contents

Foreword

In the mid-eighteenth century, the Quaker mystic and prophet John Woolman began his spiritual journal with these words: "I have often felt a motion of love to leave some hints in writing of my experience of the goodness of God."

Marcelle Martin, a Quaker mystic and prophet of the twenty-first century, has felt a motion of love to leave in writing her experience of the goodness of God, and through her eyes we are invited into a mystical journey that is at the core of the Quaker path.

This book begins where all spiritual journeys begin, with longing for God, for the More, for Truth, the Real, the Ground of Being, or whatever inadequate name we use for the Eternal Mystery. And as that inward journey deepens, it will be reflected and actualized in an outward journey of witness and resistance to the values that rule the world.

Marcelle dispels at least one myth about mystical paths, that they are solitary esoteric journeys of the individual soul. She shows us that while deeply personal, they are also deeply communal. Mystics and prophets need a community of accountability to guide and shepherd them. But she also reveals that institutions and communities may not always understand or support them, and they often need to live on the edge of the community to which they belong or call home. Marcelle understands and interprets early Quaker experience in fresh and profound ways because she has lived their journey in her inimitable way. She does not write about the early Friends as a detached historian, analytical theologian, or objective outside observer but as an intuitive, empathic fellow traveler because she shares their spiritual DNA. She enters into their story with empathy, thus parting the veil for the modern reader to cross the threshold into the profound realm of those early Quakers who lived a life of holiness and perfection. She helps us moderns understand how "perfection," the early Quaker term for transformation, comes about through the radical surrender of the self to the loving embrace of God. She provides a simple yet perennial roadmap of the way to divine union of early Friends. She also displays a gift for telling the inspiring stories of modern Friends, who continue to flesh out that roadmap with new language in different social and political contexts.

On a personal note, reading *Our Life Is Love* affected me in a two-fold manner. Although I have been a Quaker and have studied Quakerism for over half my life, I felt as though I was a mere beginner on the Quaker spiritual journey. And yet, I also felt I was being invited into the depths of other Friends' journeys as I heard echoes of my own experience, which made my own ordinary life seem more mystical.

You too may recognize yourself in many of the stages (or pathways) that are described. Although they are presented as a deepening path, Marcelle also reminds us that the stages are rarely sequential and never complete. The journey will be repeated many times, for it is a never-ending ascent (and descent), and we will return to the beginning again and again.

I am particularly excited by the passionate optimism of this book. Marcelle has a sure, strong leading that Quakers today are to play a significant role in the healing of the world, a surprising role for a religious group that is small and hidden. But she has received a clear calling, and leadings that have been unfolding for years, which she follows with a holy obedience that is awe-inspiring to more timid souls. Marcelle desires to renew the prophetic voice among Friends with a witness that is rooted in the deeply grounded spiritual journey that transformed and empowered early Friends into mystics and prophets who "turned the world upside down."

This book you hold in your hands can build a holy bridge among all branches and traditions of Friends who have the courage to walk across it, so please pass it on! It will also capture the imagination of spiritual seekers of all faiths, far beyond the bounds of the Religious Society of Friends, for the spiritual journey Marcelle describes is not limited to any one tradition.

May your encounter with *Our Life Is Love* surprise you with new and fresh insights into the spirituality of early Friends and reveal hidden moments in your own journey, which may begin to look more and more mystical.

Carole Spencer

Introduction

You will seek me and find me, when you seek me with all your heart. —Jeremiah 29:13 RSV

During my twenties, I felt a great longing to understand the truth about life. What was the purpose of human existence? Would my consciousness persist after death? Was God real? One night during a time of wholehearted seeking, while walking under a sky filled with stars, my perception suddenly opened in a new way. I had a subtle but awe-inspiring awareness of a Light that flows through all things, uniting everything. In that moment, I experienced myself as part of an eternal divine Reality shining with sacredness. I felt the Light moving through my body and out my fingertips into the world, an invisible divine Power. I sensed that the divine Power that flows through everything is great enough to heal any problem on earth, no matter how terrible or daunting it might seem.

My life changed radically. I became dedicated to a spiritual path, searching inwardly for ways to know more about the awesome Light and power I had encountered. More glimpses of divine Reality followed. It was so much more vast and universal than what I had been taught to imagine as God. To gain a better understanding of what I was experiencing, I opened a Bible that had been given to me when I was twelve. I read about Hebrews and Christians of the distant past who had received guidance to undertake certain tasks, make particular journeys, and share the good news of God's nearness. I searched the library for books about more recent spiritual seekers and read about many people through the centuries who responded courageously and faithfully to a prophetic call. I sensed a resonance between their experiences and my own.

However, it seemed that most of those in Christian history who inwardly encountered God went into monasteries, especially the women. On the other hand, I felt I was being sent into the world, not out of it. When I studied the early Quaker movement, I discovered a remarkable network of seventeenth-century women and men who lived fully human lives in the world. Coming from all social classes and diverse levels of education, the first Quakers experienced a divine Light that was within them and active in the world. God was not just an idea or belief but a dynamic power they felt in their bodies as well as their minds. Not satisfied with the dry outward husk of religious observances, they learned to feed on the living substance of life with God, whom they experienced as alive within them. Transformed in remarkable ways, they embodied their faith rather than merely proclaimed it. Divine Power moved through them because they wholeheartedly gave themselves to the process of spiritual rebirth.

The early Quakers explained that they were guided by the Light of Christ within them, the divine Light that existed in the beginning, incarnated in Jesus, and animates all created beings. Looking carefully at Scripture, they found many references that described and confirmed their experience. They did not claim to have received something new, but they did claim to have rediscovered the vibrant original form of true Christian faith. At the same time, they recognized that this divine Light is active not only in Christians but also in Jews, Muslims, Native Americans, and Africans, present to everyone as an inward Teacher.

Early Friends expected to live in Paradise after death, but they also believed that God wants to bring heaven to earth and to restore the original harmony of creation in order to bring about "the peaceable kingdom." They felt called to something far more challenging than merely *believing* in Jesus. They sensed that God wanted them to be co-workers with Christ and the prophets in bringing love, truth, equality, integrity, simplicity, justice, and peace to human relations. They allowed the saving power of the life, death, and transforming grace of Christ to *become active within themselves,* and they took seriously the biblical call to grow into the spiritual fullness that Jesus demonstrated, the call to be born anew as sons and daughters of God. With support from one another, they changed from being people conformed to their society and out of touch with God to people filled with the Spirit and wholeheartedly responsive to divine promptings.

Once they learned how to undergo the rigors of an inward, spiritual faith, they manifested God's Spirit in outward ways that transformed other people and the society around them. Calling themselves Children of Light, hundreds of the first Quakers were empowered to speak prophetically in public places and to become traveling ministers. Thousands more witnessed to their faith in ways we describe today as civil disobedience—refusing to obey laws they considered contrary to God's will and willingly suffering the legal and social consequences. Their prophetic witness in England and the colonies contributed to far-reaching religious and social changes.

Studying the writings and the lives of early Quakers and tracing their continuing impact in human history has taught me a great deal about how the Spirit is leading me and others in our own time. But it was through joining in spiritual community with Friends *today* that I learned to live the Quaker way. I have participated for over two decades now in the simple but powerful Quaker practices of deep listening, meeting for worship, discernment, and corporate decision-making. I have benefited enormously from being part of a spiritual community that recognizes that ministry takes many forms and that all are called to minister to others. I have also been helped by the example, teaching, and prayerful presence of many wise Quaker elders. Among Friends, I have found the companionship of others who have also been touched by direct experiences of God and who are attempting to live faithful, prophetic lives according to divine guidance. We have been learning together how to hear and respond wholeheartedly to God's call in our time.

I have traveled to Quaker meetings, gatherings, and retreat centers across the United States to share what I

3

have experienced and to learn from others. I spent several years as resident Quaker Studies teacher at Pendle Hill retreat center and more years living near Earlham School of Religion, a Quaker seminary. I have met Quakers from all over the world and experienced the various forms that Quakerism takes in our time. In the nineteenth century, Quakerism split into several branches, different expressions of the Quaker faith. Most branches, but not all, still identify as clearly Christian, with a focus on the experience of Christ, known within and through the Scriptures. Both "conservative" and "liberal" Quakers hold meetings for worship based in silence. During the silence, we wait expectantly to collectively experience the inward Presence and teaching of God and Christ. In the silence, any Friend present may feel a prompting from the divine Spirit to offer vocal ministry. When a message is ripe to offer, the Friend stands and speaks it aloud. This ministry is received in the silence, in which each person present discerns how the Spirit may be speaking to his or her particular heart and situation through the words that were offered.

Two branches of Quakerism in the world today, known as Friends United Meeting (FUM) and Evangelical Friends Church International (EFCI), now hold their meetings for worship in a different manner. Most of them have paid pastors who offer a Bible-based sermon during the course of their worship services. In addition, there are Scripture readings, community prayers, and singing by the congregation and by a choir. Such Quakers, also called "pastoral" or "programmed" Friends, now constitute the majority of Quakers in the world. Although the outward form of worship varies, Quakers across the theological spectrum still experience the kinds of transformation described by the first Friends and by Quakers throughout the centuries.

For a decade I felt drawn to spend considerable time reading accounts of the origins of Quakerism. I sought to understand the turbulent social context in which it arose, a period when a fresh examination of Scriptures and new religious ideas contributed to the English Civil War. The beheading of King Charles I in 1649 and a temporary experiment in a new form of government, the English Commonwealth, encouraged apocalyptic expectations. Many people experienced God breaking into history and bringing about something new. It was a fertile period for engaging in bold spiritual seeking. Quakers offered a powerfully prophetic message in this dynamic time. I was drawn to learn about not only the most well-known early Quaker leaders, such as George Fox and Margaret Fell, but also about dozens of other Friends from all social classes and many walks of life. I grew up in the late twentieth century, another time of significant social change and widespread seeking for direct spiritual experience, and I found resonances between the experiences of early Friends and my own life.

My acquaintance with the lives of seventeenth-century Quakers, combined with the experiences of dedicated Quakers today, has unveiled ten essential elements in the process of spiritual transformation. These elements are strands that weave together into a strong cord. In this book I use phrases and metaphors that have been especially meaningful to Friends over the years. Most are images from Scripture that have long been alive for Quakers and descriptive of their experience.

Because I have been drawn to study the passionate beginning of the Quaker movement, half of the sections in this book focus on the experiences of Quakers in the mid-seventeenth century. However, the ten elements I describe in the Quaker spiritual journey can also be seen in the experiences of Quakers throughout the centuries since then. In different time periods, some elements have been emphasized more than others. The stories and writings of Quakers in all centuries are worth studying and have much to teach.

Many people today experience and describe the ten elements differently than the first Friends did, but in our time we are still called to make a radically transformative spiritual journey, as shown by the experiences of contemporary Quakers included in this book. Comprehending how Quakers have experienced the spiritual journey can help everyone understand and cooperate more fully with the movement of the Spirit that wants to transform the human race now, as we face the challenges of our day.

A Radical, Transforming Faith

He has granted to us his precious and very great promises, that through these you may escape from the corruption that is in the world . . . and become partakers of the divine nature. —2 Peter 1:4 RSV*

Like most of their contemporaries in England, the first Quakers were Christians. However, they fiercely challenged the mainstream Christianity of their time, which they felt had become so much a matter of form and human invention that it deadened people's spiritual sensitivity and hindered genuine spiritual discovery. Seeking truth and direct experience, early Friends discovered a spirituality that brought them more alive. In an unexpected, tangible, but non-physical way, God and Christ became real and present to them, not only transcendent but also present within and among them and active in the world. They proclaimed they had discovered the true, original form of Christianity, a faith guided directly by the living Christ, available within all people as a Light.† This Light inwardly illuminated the truth, guided their path, and empowered them to take up a new way of living. It showed them that the Spirit infused and informed every aspect of life. Their belief was founded on experience and confirmed by their reading of Scripture.

Like their contemporaries, early Quakers believed that Adam and Eve's disobedience left humanity and society in a fallen state. The Light revealed that most people, including themselves, lived in bondage to mental, social,

---

* Unless otherwise noted, all biblical quotes are from the New Revised Standard Translation (NRSV). The translations most often used by early Quakers were the Geneva Bible and King James (Authorized) Version.

† Quoting John 1:9, they insisted that the same Light which incarnated in Jesus also lights every single person: *The true light, which enlightens everyone, was coming into the world.*

and spiritual repression, largely without being aware of it. As they paid attention, they became painfully aware of their conscious and unconscious collusion with the deception and oppression built into the structure of their society. They saw that their participation in certain social norms and practices caused them to be false and inauthentic.

Although early Friends believed in "the Fall," they testified to a process of restoration and rebirth that frees people of their fallen nature. For them, the Bible was literally true, but they also understood Scripture stories as metaphors that reveal powerful spiritual truths. Humanity originally lived in a state of paradisiacal unity with God and all creation. Human beings, female as well as male, had originally been created in the divine image: *So God created humankind in his image, in the image of God he created them; male and female he created them* (Genesis 1:27).

Thus, the first humans were created with a divine nature. When Adam and Eve began to "feed on" the knowledge of good and evil, however, their divine nature became obscured and corrupted. Early Quakers identified the problem not only as disobedience to God but also as a feeding of the intellect to the neglect of experiential awareness of God's Presence and guidance. A contemporary reading might add that humanity fell out of its original awareness of the oneness of all things and became dominated by the desires and fears inherent in a physical state divorced from spiritual perception.

Being remade and restored to the original divine nature requires fierce truthfulness both about one's inner life and about one's behavior and participation in society. It demands surrendering control to God and submitting to the death of the old self, a humbling process that the fearful part of each person resists tenaciously. Following inward guidance, step by faithful step, however, the lives of early Friends changed, both within and without. Through their collective love of the inward, guiding Light of Christ,

8

and with the support of the community, great numbers of early Friends learned to respond faithfully to the divine call. As they did so, they experienced God's Refining Fire cleansing and purifying them within.

Early Friends believed that the eternal Word of God (the Light) was bringing about reconciliation and restoring humanity to its original, pure condition. Many of them testified to the spiritual rebirth that Jesus described when he said, *"Very truly, I tell you, no one can see the kingdom of God without being born from above"* (John 3:3). As they awakened to Christ within, they gradually became liberated from social conformity and gave witness to a new way of life. Those who fully offered up their lives became inwardly united with God, whom they sometimes referred to as the Fountain of Love; they experienced divine Love flowing through them to others. These Friends regarded their experience as fulfillment of the promise in 2 Peter 1:4 that followers of Christ would be liberated from the corruption of the world's ways and would become *partakers of the divine nature.*

The writings of early Quakers include many references to Romans 8:14: *For as many as are led by the Spirit of God, they are the sons of God* (KJV). Early in the Quaker movement, when their language was the most radical, they sometimes referred to themselves as Sons of God, occasionally using the more inclusive phrase Sons and Daughters of God.[1] History shows that thousands of the first Quakers were transformed into wholehearted, courageous agents of major social changes, changes that are still helping to liberate people today. Looking in greater depth at how early Quakers experienced spiritual rebirth may help people today—people of every form of faith— learn to cooperate with the extraordinary spiritual transformation that is being called forth from all of us now, as we encounter the challenges of our time.

Ten Elements of the Journey

The Spirit-filled movement of early Quakerism demonstrates how a community collectively surrendering to the inward Light of Christ can actively participate in the divine transformation of human society, making divine Love and Truth more tangible and visible. This book expands upon ten elements of the spiritual journey experienced by the first Quakers and by Friends in our time. These elements have been grouped into three sections: Awakening, Convincement, and Faithfulness. This suggests a linear process, and, indeed, we experience certain elements more intensely at different stages. However, each of the elements, like strands of thread in a tapestry, weaves throughout the journey.

For each of the ten elements, examples are given of how both seventeenth-century and contemporary Quakers have experienced them. Friends in recent times have been influenced by their exposure to many systems of religious thought, and some of the language we use to explain our experiences reflects this. Our way of understanding and describing our experiences is not uniform. Still, we experience the same elements of the spiritual journey. Our metaphors point to a spiritual reality too vast to define in words. Although early Friends developed a particular way of describing these elements, the spiritual journey they described has been experienced by many other individuals and groups in Christian history.

Awakening

God is present always and everywhere. Many have glimpses of this, especially in childhood. There comes a time, however, when the need to know about the life of the Spirit takes central importance in a person's life. Thus begins a conscious spiritual journey.

Longing in the Seventeenth Century

Early Quaker accounts of the spiritual journey contain striking descriptions of an intense longing to know God, often starting in childhood. Both William Dewsbury and George Fox, for example, while working as shepherds in their youth, brought Bibles with them into the fields. During long hours spent outdoors, they read Scripture and prayed. Sarah Blackborow wrote that from childhood she experienced, "pure breathings and desires, and thirstings after God."[2] She described the condition of many in her time "who are in the pantings and thirst, whose hearts are breathing after the living God, in whom desires have been begotten by the eternal spirit."[3] Such spiritual thirst affected people of all social classes.

The longing of many was felt as a desire to be accepted or "owned" by God. When she was in her teens, heiress Mary Springett (later Penington) yearned to know the right, true way to pray. She zealously tried many ways to do so. Being acceptable to God was more important than anything money could buy, and her longing increased as she grew older. In her spiritual autobiography she wrote:

> Oh! the groans and cries in secret that were raised in me, that I might be visited of the Lord, and come to the knowledge of his way; and that my feet might be turned into that way, before I went hence. . . . I would cry out: "I care not for [an inheritance] in this life: give it to those who care for it. I am miserable with it: it is acceptance with thee I desire and that alone can satisfy me."[4]

Margaret Fell wrote that from the time of her marriage she was "desirous to serve God, so that I might be accepted [by] him."[5]

During the mid-seventeenth century, there was a great deal of preaching about human sinfulness. Calvinist preachers taught that sinful behavior was a sign that one was predestined to eternal damnation. Even children were burdened by a sense that much of their behavior was displeasing to God. In his boyhood, Stephen Crisp could see that he was more careful than other children and less profane. Nonetheless, he felt unable to stop delighting in vanity and doing things he judged not to be innocent. He developed a strong desire for the power to overcome this sinfulness:

> I wanted power to answer the requirings of that in me, which witnesseth against evil in me, and this I lamented day and night. And when I was about nine or ten years old, I sought the power of God with great diligence and earnestness, with strong cries and tears; and if I had had the whole world I would have given it, to have known how to obtain power over my corruptions.[6]

Old and young, seventeenth-century people were terrified of being predestined to hell, and they despaired when they were unable to stop committing acts that they judged sinful or that their conscience witnessed to be wrong.

They had been taught that God was in a distant heaven beyond the earth and that Christ was far away, way out there in a resurrected physical body. They longed for God to be close, and, even more so, they longed to be acceptable to God. Many felt a deep yearning to know the true way to worship and how to live a holy life, subjects about which there was a great deal of debate in their time. Joan Vokins often cried out in prayer, "Lord reveal thy Way unto me, that I may walk therein, whatever I undergo."[7]

Sometimes the longing to know God and God's way was coupled with a painful awareness of the hypocrisy, corruption, and injustice in society. George Fox was disgusted that so many who "professed" to be Christians acted in shameful ways, from the cousin who wanted him to participate in a beer-drinking contest to the judge who acted unjustly. He called these people "professors" because they *professed* to be Christians but did not act like Christians should. He longed to meet those who had come into true inward "possession" of their faith.

Longing in Our Time

During the time of the early Friends, religious belief and observance was pervasive. In the twentieth century, however, it became increasingly common for people not to adhere to a particular faith. Even many contemporary Friends who were brought up without religious beliefs, however, have experienced a longing for spiritual truth. Paula Deming was raised to be agnostic and was taught to "sneer at religion." When she was in her twenties, however, a powerful feeling took hold:

> *I began to experience a sense of doom, that what we strive for in this material world wasn't enough to satisfy me. But what else was there, other than what I was taught? You might say I experienced longing for meaning beyond the limits that I had learned. Because religion was not acceptable for me, and God was to be despised, my spiritual journey began with fear. I had no language to describe my feelings, and this 'longing for meaning' manifested itself as a feeling that someone/thing was chasing me. Only little by little did I find mention and understanding of things spiritual . . . and this gave me a little leap of joy—a sense of Truth. This unfolding took a long time, and it required much sharing with others, both for affirmation of my experiences and for acceptance of my spiritual unfolding. I was very frightened that my husband and friends would find me unacceptable.[8]*

Lola Georg was awakened by a painful period in her life,

> *when despair, tragedy, and trauma had dropped me to my knees. I did not necessarily see at the time that I was longing to seek a spiritual relationship with the Divine, rather I was looking to alleviate the pain I felt inside. Thinking that there must be something more than the pain and suffering I was feeling, I turned to God with a "what could it hurt?" attitude.*[9]

For many Friends in our time, longing is first experienced as dissatisfaction with the ways of the world and a vague sense that we are meant to live in a better way. As a child, Margaret Hope Bacon sometimes sensed a nurturing divine Presence with her. In her teenage years, however, financial misfortune caused her parents to move from a northern city, where she had been thriving in a progressive school, to a racially segregated southern state. The injustice and cruelty she witnessed there shocked her, and she could not understand why others around her did not express the same compassion and outrage she felt. In spite of her uneasiness with reciting a creed, she began attending church:

> *In frustration I turned to the local Episcopal Church, hoping to find at least some statement of moral values. At Young People's [Fellowship], made up primarily of social misfits like myself, I blossomed. . . . I was able to talk about racism, though in the most general of terms. . . . We had a wonderful priest at our local church, a saintly man who believed in practicing the presence of God. Through his help I was able to surmount problems of doubt and give myself up to the worship.*[10]

In Western culture, the lack of closeness to God that is felt by many is fostered by an internal split between the head and the heart. A sense of dryness and anguish covers a longing for God. Steve Smith was raised Quaker in Iowa.

14

As a child he felt "awe and wonder" when hearing stories from the Bible. As he grew, however, his "inchoate longings were aimless or else diverted into the elaborate byways of analytic philosophy, which tantalized but never satisfied."[11] For many years, pursuing academic success by studying philosophy covered over the rift between his head and heart:

> Driven by unrelenting self-expectations, I had climbed an apparently ascending path through college and graduate school into my first full-time teaching appointment and marriage. Each success, each award and public recognition brought private depression in its wake, however, as I once again discovered that the peace of mind and self-acceptance I craved could not be earned by excelling in the games of learning I had chosen to pursue. Still, I knew no other way. . . . Years of academic skepticism had corroded the naïve faith of my childhood; I trusted only my intellect.[12]

Smith dealt with the painful split between head and heart by drinking alcohol to excess. In spite of his marriage to a talented woman, the birth of a son, and success in his career, this drinking became an increasing problem. Finally, prodded by a doctor, he entered therapy and "began the long, hard road to recovery." First, he replaced one addiction with another. This only led to greater isolation and deeper depression. Then, he broadened his philosophical vision beyond the scope of his previous studies, which he realized had been "technical and precise . . . distrustful of larger questions of meaning and value." A deep longing motivated him to study how to find happiness and well-being.

A few Friends today have always been blessedly aware of the presence of God. Michael Gibson, for example, maintained this awareness since childhood. It was nurtured by the church he attended:

I cannot remember not having the God connection. Even when I was four and five years old I remember being consciously in relationship with God, and it was, in part, the established church that fed and nurtured that relationship. True, some of the church's teachings and practices have been at odds with my experience at nearly every stage of my life, but I was somehow able to know—I don't know how, it was a gift—that those teachings and practices were not the point, not the content of my faith, but were human expressions of faith. The Life down deep, the living sap, was the point. And I believe I always knew it was flowing in me.[13]

Some find that their longing for a deeper spirituality increases once they have glimpsed the divine Presence in their lives. Jessica Easter's awakening felt like a seduction, in which God was

seducing me into a deeper walk with Her by offering small tastes of what union with Her is like. That seduction has taken me into the farthest depths of myself and the strangest corners of the world. I was hooked. I still am hooked.[14]

Awakening to the spiritual journey often begins with some form of longing, sometimes felt as dissatisfaction with the way things are. Longing remains as a strand of the journey even after one finds a connection with God.

Reflection Questions

Longing

In what form have you experienced longing or a desire for deeper meaning and purpose?

Do you long for deeper knowledge or connection with God?

If you haven't felt longing, have you experienced restlessness, cynicism, or despair about the way things are?

What have you done with your longing or your sense that something is wrong or missing?

Can you remember a recent time when you felt a desire for greater connection with God or longed to live a life with greater love and integrity?

Seeking in the Seventeenth Century

Strong longing compels people to seek a way to come closer to the heart of life, to love and truth and God. In 1646 young George Fox began his search by looking for a wise priest or minister who could teach him the way. Like others who eventually became the first Quakers, he attended the sermons and lectures of priests and ministers who had a reputation for spiritual wisdom, traveling long distances to do so. In mid-seventeenth-century England, there was increased freedom for spiritual exploration, and many "nonconformist" clergy were preaching new religious ideas. Only a few decades earlier, the Bible had finally become available in English in a small edition inexpensive enough for ordinary people to afford. The Bible was often the only book that families owned; they read passages aloud together during daily times for prayer.

For decades, those called Puritans had wanted to purify the church of rituals not mentioned in the Scriptures; many of them refused to conform to such practices. Numerous religious groups sprang up, each with a slightly different idea about what constituted a true, pure church. All the Puritan groups in England put emphasis on finding instructions in Scripture about what God wanted. However, the different sects had fierce debates over scriptural interpretations. Those dissatisfied with the state-run church, longing to find a truer way to worship God, joined the new religious sects. They read devotional or theological books, attended midweek lectures, and took up spiritual practices such as fasting. On Sundays they participated in long morning and afternoon worship services and abstained from sports and card playing. The more radical non-conformists were called Independents, Separatists, Dissenters, and Anabaptists. Their descendants today include Presbyterians, Congregationalists, and Baptists.

Hearing there were strict Puritans in Leeds, Yorkshire teenager William Dewsbury persuaded his family to apprentice him to someone in that town. At Sunday services, he sang psalms, took communion, and wrote down the sermons in shorthand. During the week he fasted and participated in all the other recommended practices. When he had free time, he visited ministers in their homes and asked for clarification of various points they had made while preaching. These educated ministers, however, responded solely from their book learning. They did not speak of any direct knowledge of God. Not one was able to describe to young Dewsbury any personal experience of God that had enabled them to overcome sin:

> I met with none who could tell me what God had done for their souls, in redeeming them from the body of sin, which I groaned under, and which separated me from the presence of God; although I walked strictly with them in their outward observances and in running to hear one man after another, called ministers, yet I found no rest nor peace to my weary soul.[15]

In London, Martha Simmonds, daughter of a family of printers, engaged in a similar search. Wanting to find a minister who spoke truth, she attended a variety of religious services and meetings held in public places or in people's homes. In spite of all she heard preached by many ministers about God and religion, she, too, was unable to find what she was seeking:

> For seven years together I wandered up and down the streets enquiring of those that had the image of honesty in their countenances, where I might find an honest Minister . . . and wandering from one idol's temple to another, and from one private meeting to another, I heard a sound of words among them but no substance could I find.[16]

When Elizabeth Hooton, a farmer's wife, found the services at the local Anglican church inadequate for her spiritual needs, she joined a group of General Baptists. At that time the Baptists—also called Anabaptists—were on the radical end of the Puritan spectrum. They believed that baptism was only for mature believers, not infants. In their services they allowed the ministry of lay preachers, sometimes even women. When many of the Baptists Elizabeth Hooton had joined lost the heart to continue their religious observances, she judged that they "were not upright hearted to ye Lord but did his work negligently."[17] She gathered the remnants of the shattered group and held meetings in her house in the village of Skegby, sometimes preaching to the group. Her husband was unhappy about this, and the marriage nearly broke up. Nonetheless, Elizabeth Hooton continued the meetings, and her children attended them.

In the rural north of England, Francis Howgill had been seeking for decades. He sometimes had intimations of God, felt divine Power, or received inner guidance. However, these manifestations of the Spirit were subtle and not in the form he expected an appearance from God to take. Not recognizing the source, he usually paid little attention and often neglected to heed the guidance that came. His family and friends did not understand his spiritual longing, and Howgill felt a deep loneliness. Joining a succession of churches, he was moved by the tender sincerity of each group. Eventually, however, they all disappointed him. They were focused on understanding the words of Scripture and talked only about what God and Christ had done in the past. They did not know the living God or the risen Christ by direct experience. Howgill wrote:

> I fasted and prayed and walked mournfully in sorrow, and thought none was like me, tempted on every hand. So I ran to this man and the other, and they made promises to me, but it was only words. . . . Then there appeared more beauty in them called Independents, and I loved them, and so joined them. And I purchased books with all the money that I could get, and walked with them and owned them as more separate

from the world. . . . But at last I saw it was but in words. . . . They whom they called Anabaptists appeared to have more glory and walked more according to scripture, observing things written without. And I went among them and there was something I loved about them. But . . . I saw the ground was the same, and their doctrine out of the life, with the rest of the teachers of the world, and they had separated themselves and made another likeness. But still all said, the letter [of scripture] was the word and rule, and Christ at a distance without, had done all; and some of them holding freewill, others opposing, and all in [their own] will. But still I loved them and walked honestly among all these; but though I had seen and owned all that I had heard . . . no peace nor no guide did I find.[18]

Seeking in Our Time

Douglas Gwyn describes two different kinds of "seeker tendencies" that emerged in the second half of the twentieth century in the United States and Europe, at a time when dialogue among Christian denominations had increased as well as access to knowledge of other world religions. One kind of seeker left the mainstream Christian or Jewish faith in which they had been raised, seeking "more adequate answers and authorities" by exploring Buddhist, Hindu, Native American or earth-based "pagan" religious practices.[19] Another kind of seeker stayed within the religious tradition of their upbringing but sought for deeper experience of the truths at the heart of their religion, exploring new practices or visiting different denominations. "Thus," Gwyn wrote, "even traditionalists became seekers, forced to search for new ways to convey old truths."[20] Some seekers tried one route, then the other.

Louise Wilson's seeking took her deeper within her own spiritual tradition. She was raised in North Carolina among "progressive Quakers," whose worship services included songs and a prepared message. As a child she attended Sunday school, memorized Bible verses, and learned important values from her loving parents. After her marriage she felt called to seek for a deeper life with God:

> *My conscious spiritual journey began in the fall of 1952. The children were in school, Bob was at work and I had time to look at myself and I didn't like what I saw. I had my social life, my intellectual life, and my religious life. I was many persons, not one, and I continued in a pattern, not liking it, but making no changes.*[21]

Finally she began to read the Bible and books of a spiritual nature. Then she joined an interdenominational prayer group.

Timothy Ashworth was led to seek outside the tradition in which he was raised. The son of an Anglican priest, his upbringing made him sensitive to the religious life, but he sought for a vitality he didn't find inside the church. First he attended a school of meditation and took up an Eastern meditation practice involving a mantra. This practice helped him be more present throughout the day. Desiring more, he began to attend Catholic services and soon was discussing theological questions with the priest and reading books on religion. Both meditation practice and attending Mass helped him experience "a tangible spaciousness and depth of presence."[22] He joined the Roman Catholic Church, went to seminary, earned a degree in Scripture studies, and was ordained as a priest.

Still, his seeking continued. A conversation with a meditation teacher led him to make a commitment to surrender one hundred percent to God, something he felt a priest should do. Shortly afterwards, he experienced an overwhelming, sweet, fiery sensation in his heart, along with a powerful shift in consciousness. The experience continued for weeks and reoriented his entire life. As he surrendered to the presence of God within him, he was led, surprisingly, to leave the priesthood. Later, he married a woman he had known in college and went to Oxford for more studies. When his wife brought him to a Quaker meeting, he began to read about the beginnings of Quakerism, finding a resonance between the experience of early Friends and his own transforming encounter with God.

Deborah Saunders's grandmother was a devout Southern Baptist married to a devout Episcopalian. Hers was one of the few African American families who attended the Episcopalian church in which she was raised. When her daughter was six, Saunders felt hungry for a more personal relationship with God and joined a fundamentalist church. Although they were the only black members of the congregation, they felt welcome. In this community, Saunders read the Scriptures and reached her own understanding of what they meant and what she believed as a Christian. Then she felt God leading her to another place of worship: "I heard that still, small voice within telling me to continue my quest."[23] She joined a black Pentecostal church, where she felt a powerful sense of fellowship and spiritual renewal.

> *I was caught in a spiritual awakening much like Paul on his way to Damascus. It was my first experience in an all-African American community of faith, and I knew it was where I was supposed to be. My daughter was young, my family was miles away, and God had placed me in a church that embraced me not only as a member of the church, but also as a member of the church family.*[24]

Saunders became the assistant youth director. Seven years later, when she heard the inner call to move to another faith community, she rebelled, and "it took more than a year before I yielded my will in holy obedience."[25] When she finally spoke with the pastor, he recommended she try a Quaker meeting. The following Sunday she found herself sitting in silence in a small New Jersey meeting among a handful of people, most of them her elders. On that day, and on subsequent Sundays, she heard "the still, small voice within" saying to her, "This is the time in your journey, dear child, that you must learn to be still and know that I am God."[26] Although Saunders had never experienced anything like this kind of silent worship before, she found peace. She began to see more clearly the nature of the path on which God was leading her. "At each juncture of my journey I clearly see the lessons learned. At this time, God has chosen the Religious Society of Friends as the place for me to affirm my faith and put it into practice."[27]

Many Quakers today, whether or not they were raised Christian, find that their spiritual seeking leads them beyond Christianity before bringing them to find their spiritual home among Friends. In boarding school, Alex Wildwood was forced to attend religious services where readings from Scripture were used as the basis for boring and intellectually insulting lectures. This caused him to view Christianity as "a religion of shoulds and oughts, a prescriptive faith morbidly obsessed with sacrifice and suffering."[28] Taught to prize rationality, he became a skeptical, self-reliant atheist. It was in nature that he found solace. Among plants and animals he was aware of "an awesome, mysterious power at work."[29] During the Vietnam war, he engaged in radical social critique and participated in student protests against the military-industrial complex. After the birth of his first child, and through feminist women he knew, he became involved in pagan outdoor religious ceremonies that honored the cycles of life and death, the seasons and the land, celebrating "our embeddedness in the sacred web of life." Wildwood was influenced by Buddhist scholar and environmental activist Joanna Macy, a person with a prophetic message. Don't get lost in the distractions of the addictive consumer culture, she taught. Instead, face the pain of really seeing how we are devastating the planet; make the choice to be "conscious."

In his late thirties, Wildwood went to live in an East London community started by Quakers, most of them activists, and he began attending a Quaker meeting. He liked how Quakers offered an alternative to society's emphasis on extreme individualism. Friends seemed more "strongly committed to the practical relief of suffering in this world, rather than [to] theological speculation about some heavenly realm to come."[30] He recognized that something internal had been nudging him toward the Quaker community. He also found additional needed companionship when he became involved in Twelve Step fellowships for addiction recovery. In both Quakerism and in the Twelve Step programs, he found a common commitment to "the surrendered life."

Timothy Ashworth and Alex Wildwood, representing the two different kinds of seekers described by Gwyn, have engaged in a dialogue at Woodbrooke, England's Quaker study center. Ashworth found deep meaning in Christianity and traditional church services but was drawn to seek the depths of the Christian mystery, the essence of Christian faith. In contrast, Wildwood's negative early experiences in Christian churches caused him to seek spirituality elsewhere—in nature, in recognition of the sacredness of the earth, in community, and in activism. Now, his engagement as a Friend has led him to explore the Christian roots of Quakerism.

Reflection Questions

Seeking

How have you sought for spiritual knowledge or meaning in life?

At what times and in what ways have you sought outside yourself for greater spiritual understanding or communion with God?

What kinds of thoughts, feelings, desires, fears, or intuitions motivate you to seek?

Does the tradition of your upbringing satisfy you or have you explored outside that tradition?

In what ways have you been a seeker?

Has your seeking borne fruit?

Turning Within in the Seventeenth Century

Many people were seekers for years or decades before they became the first Quakers. For varying periods of time, they had found a place in the churches of their day, engaging seriously in the practices of each denomination they joined. Eventually, however, they recognized they still felt painfully disconnected from God. Many had expected a glorious Second Coming. A Civil War in England and the beheading of King Charles I had raised expectations that a more godly form of government would soon be established, but the new Puritan government failed to create the holy new society for which many had hoped. Shameful political wrangling and intrigue continued as before, and a general malaise spread across England. Society was still corrupt, and Christ still seemed very distant. Many people, continuing to feel burdened by a sense of their sinfulness, concluded they had not found the living faith for which they yearned. They saw no promising alternatives in the world around them. Disillusionment came suddenly for some and slowly for others. In 1650 Isaac Penington wrote,

> *If ever there was a time for tears without, and a grief of spirit within, this seems the season . . . when after such an expectation of Light and Glory, of settlement and establishment in the things of God, such thick darkness, such universal shame, such dreadful shatterings, have so apparently overtaken us, and are so likely daily more and more to overtake us.*[31]

Only after giving up hope of finding what they were seeking outwardly did many begin to sense that help was available within. In London, Martha Simmonds had some brief glimpses of a spiritual light that made her feel she was wasting her time attending various churches and meetings, pursuing men with scholarly knowledge. Instead, she needed to wait quietly and attend to what was happening within: "[At] about the end of seven years hunting and finding no rest, the Lord opened a little glimmering of light

27

to me . . . and then for about seven years more he kept me still."[32] During this period, she waited at home for more light to be revealed.

For years, young Mary Springett and her husband had tried out various Separatist churches and engaged in zealous prayer and Puritan practices. William Springett poured his financial resources into supporting the Puritan Army during the Civil War. When he died, his widow redoubled her spiritual efforts, but she did not feel any nearness to God. After the death of her baby son, she finally stopped attending services or following prescribed practices, not wanting to be drawn in by any more vain boasts of purity or false promises of spiritual attainment. She prayed at home and waited for a true revelation from God. Some remarkable dreams suggested that one day her prayers would be answered. In one dream, she met Christ, come among ordinary people and wearing plain clothes.

After spending years traveling to hear the most renowned Anglican priests and Puritan ministers in England, George Fox was still unable to find anyone who could tell him about God or Christ from direct experience. After he finally gave up hope of finding help from other people, he had intimations that he could be taught directly, inwardly. He found support for this in Scripture:

> *But the anointing which ye have received of him abideth in you, and ye need not that any man teach you: but as the same anointing teacheth you of all things, and is truth, and is no lie, and even as it hath taught you, ye shall abide in him.*
> (1 John 2:27 KJV)

The young man stopped roaming and went home. His parents were displeased, however, that he would not attend church with them. Instead, he spent his time looking inward. Later he wrote:

> *I fasted much, and walked abroad in solitary places many days, and often took my Bible and went and sat in hollow trees and lonesome places*

till night came on; and frequently in the night walked mournfully about by myself, for I was a man of sorrows in the times of the first workings of the Lord in me. . . . I kept myself much as a stranger, seeking heavenly wisdom and getting knowledge from the Lord, and was brought off from outward things to rely wholly on the Lord alone. And though my exercises and troubles were very great, yet were they not so continual but that I had some intermissions, and was sometimes brought into such an heavenly joy that I thought I had been in Abraham's bosom.[33]

After he discovered Christ present within as an inward Light and Teacher, Fox traveled to share this good news in towns and villages across England, wearing the sturdy leather pants and jacket of an itinerant laborer. In the little village of Skegby, he met Elizabeth Hooton. The farmer's wife understood the young man's spiritual condition better than anyone else had done. She listened eagerly to the revelations he had received inwardly from Christ. Fox preached to her small group of General Baptists that they, too, could be taught directly by the Spirit, which was present within them as a Light, the same Light that *lighteth every man that cometh into the world* (John 1:9 KJV). George Fox's message emphasized that a measure of the Light of Christ is present like a tiny seed within each person, needing careful attention and cultivation. In most souls, the seed is choked by an overabundance of worldly pursuits and desires or covered over by erroneous beliefs and practices.

Following Fox's instructions, the group that met at Elizabeth Hooton's house discovered the Light of Christ inside themselves. They began to call themselves Children of the Light, the original name for those eventually called Quakers. Later, Quakers gave themselves the name Friends in the Truth; they called each other Friends, which is what Jesus had said he would call his disciples.

29

Further north, Fox found more people ready to receive his message to look within. Some had already discovered the indwelling Presence of the living Christ. William Dewsbury and several others joined him in traveling to share the Quaker message. In the region of Westmoreland, hundreds of people called Seekers had been waiting for a divine revelation of the true way to worship God. When they heard Fox speak, many sensed he was the person they had been waiting for, someone with the same prophetic power as the apostles.

Judge Thomas Fell and his wife, Margaret, members of the gentry, were known for welcoming traveling ministers into their home, Swarthmore Hall. When George Fox knocked on their door, Margaret Fell was taken aback by his use of the familiar pronouns "thee" and "thou." A man below her social class would normally address her by the plural "you." However, she had dreamed recently of a man wearing an unusual white hat who would come and "confound the priests."[34] She welcomed him to stay overnight in the attic. The next day, after the priest's sermon at the Ulverston church, Fox was granted permission to speak to the congregation. Margaret Fell wrote about his startling message:

> George Fox went to the Ulverston steeple-house . . . and . . . stood up upon a seat or form, and . . . said: "Christ [is] the Light of the world, and lighteth every man that cometh into the world; and . . . by this light [we] might be gathered to God." And I stood up in my pew and wondered at his doctrine, for I had never heard such before. And then he went on and opened the Scriptures and said: "The Scriptures [are] the prophet's words, and Christ's and the apostles' words, and what as they spoke, they enjoyed and possessed, and had it from the Lord. Then what had any to do with the Scriptures, but as they came to the Spirit that gave them forth? You will say, Christ saith this, and the apostles say this, but what

canst thou say? Art thou a child of Light, and hast thou walked in the Light, and what thou speakest, is it inwardly from God?"[35]

Although people had often praised Margaret Fell for her piety, she suddenly recognized she had been living a second-hand religion. Unlike the authors of Scripture, she did not know Christ directly and could not speak of God from personal knowledge. Fox's message was piercing:

It cut me to the Heart; and then I saw clearly, we were all wrong. So I sat down in my Pew again, and cried bitterly: and I cried in my Spirit to the Lord, We are all Thieves, we are all Thieves; we have taken the Scripture in Words, and know nothing of them in ourselves.[36]*

Fell began to spend time in silent worship, waiting to have direct experience of God and Christ. Soon she became one of many early Quakers who shared the message of the inward Christ in writing and through spoken testimony.

Turning Within in Our Time

Sometimes people turn within as a natural movement in a gradually deepening spiritual life. When Louise Wilson first felt the need for a more unified life, she attended a prayer group and read books. At the time her family moved to a new location, her spiritual life moved to a deeper place, a place of inward listening for the still, small voice of God: "Finally I began to get up an hour before anyone else was awakened. I read Scripture. I prayed. I waited upon the Lord, and I made notes on thoughts that seemed important."[37]

---

* Spelling, punctuation, and capitalization were not standard in the seventeenth century. I have made a few changes to these in some of the quotes by early Quakers to make their writing more accessible to contemporary readers, while retaining enough of the original to give a flavor of their texts.

Many people only look within when crisis or despair leaves no alternative source of help. Troubling experiences can be an invitation or pathway to discovering God's inward Presence and activity. Bolivian teenager Raúl Choque Mamani read the entire Bible by the age of fourteen. Then he had a crisis of faith, during which he was plagued by questions

> about the existence of God, the validity of the dogmas, and the role played by Christianity throughout history. All of these questions led to doubt and skepticism, such that I ultimately became an atheist.[38]

His new heroes were Marxist revolutionary leaders. He suffered from nightmares, however, and developed a distressing physical pain in his neck. Choque Mamani began to read arguments for the existence of God but still continued to have doubts and troubling dreams. Each night he said the prayer, "Lord God, I don't know if you exist; if you exist I would like you to help me to leave this very difficult situation in which I find myself."[39] Day after day, week after week, he waited for clarity and healing.

Kenyan Priscilla Makhino was raised in a Quaker family and attended Quaker schools. After her father died in her childhood, she began to spend time outdoors in prayer. In the woods she "experienced God's first touch."[40] However, even though she continued to regularly participate in church services, her childhood experiences of God's Presence gave way to challenges, doubts, and fears as she became an adult. She experienced a long, painful sickness. She asked her pastor for prayers, but nothing improved. For many years she felt she was

> in the deep and shut up. . . . My sorrows, troubles, pain, and temptations were so great that I despaired and waited for death to come. All this time I never turned to God for help. But I continued to trust and rely on mankind.[41]

After a doctor refused to operate on a painful condition that she feared would kill her, Makhino spent a night alone in a dark room. There she had a vision of three men dressed in white singing, "You should never be discouraged. Take it to the Lord in prayer!" The vision penetrated the thick veil of fear that had been troubling her for years, and she became attentive to God's Presence in a new way:

> This created hope in me for the first time after fifteen years of despair. I woke very early in the morning . . . and headed for home to start a new kind of life. I said to myself, "I will seek and find this God that is Love and the Jesus that loves me." God remembered me two days later with another visitation.[42]

Charlotte Fardelmann, a mother, writer, and photographer, was active in her Quaker meeting. When she faced a painful writer's block after receiving a contract to write her first book, she looked to God for help. In her journal she wrote,

> I am always under great pressure—why? I put myself in this position—why? I'm shaking all over. I don't know who to turn to, how to get out of this position. I'm crying so hard I can hardly write. I'm screaming from the depths of my heart. Oh God . . . Where are you?[43]

One Sunday at her Quaker meeting, she stood up and asked for help. In the silence that followed, she sensed a response coming from within, a message in several parts. Inwardly, she heard that her book would be finished by the deadline, that it would be good, and that after she finished it, she needed to take time to do something different. She understood that her writer's block had been dissolved. Afterwards, words flowed. When the book was done, she felt that God had helped her complete it and now wanted her to take a four-month "spiritual sabbatical," a time dedicated to inward listening. During those months, she

33

prayed, read books, went for long walks, and noticed her dreams. After being in an automobile accident caused by her nodding off at the wheel, she arranged to spend a week at Pendle Hill, the Quaker retreat and study center in Wallingford, Pennsylvania. There, a teacher listened to her soul in a way nobody had ever done before. This woman urged Charlotte to make even more space for contemplation and told her that a week at Pendle Hill might not be enough.

Something inside Fardelmann leapt up in recognition of the truth that she needed to take more time to look within. The following year, she spent nine months as a resident student at Pendle Hill. It was a period of turning inward, and God stripped away her old self and gave birth to something new. The daily morning meetings for worship at Pendle Hill were "a time of being melted, of sitting in the Spirit and being worked on deep down."[44] During classes, daily kitchen chores, and interactions with people at meals, she was aware of paying inward attention in a new way. Daily she wrote down "thoughts, feelings, lessons learned, inner messages, and quotes I liked."[45] She reviewed her journal, making notes in different colors and drawing pictures. During a two-day silent retreat at a little hermitage on campus, she wrote, "I think God is laying hold on me. . . I feel very vulnerable like a lobster that has shed a shell and is waiting to form a new one."[46]

Stephanie Crumley-Effinger, Director of Supervised Ministry at Earlham School of Religion (ESR), struggled with great fatigue after several surgeries. Her doctor recommended Mindfulness Based Stress Reduction. This practice and other efforts to recover from her illness pushed her to turn within, in silence, in a deeper way than she had ever done before. During a sermon she delivered at ESR, she spoke about the call to empty of her self in order to be more open and available to God:

Despite being a quiet-appreciating Quaker for almost forty years, in learning mindfulness practice I discovered the extent to which, even in the silence of waiting worship or individual centering, my still body harbors a relentlessly busy mind. The call to be still and focused is a gift of many scripture passages, including, from Luke 10:41b-2a, Jesus inviting Martha to stewardship of that moment, from Mark 4:39 the story of Jesus stilling the storm, and from Psalm 46:10 the admonition to be still and know God. In these and many other sources, the Christian tradition is replete with guidance to take time from the fullness of activity and thoughts, to make room for God. For many years I had also appreciated lines from Thomas Edward Brown's poem 'Indwelling,' especially the lines "thou art all replete with very thou, and hast such shrewd activity" and being "small and full." Indeed I had often prayed to be large and spacious so that there would be more room for God. What I had failed to appreciate, though, was that my very ways of seeking God were themselves part of being small and full and "replete with very thou." I had largely mastered the first level of being able to sit quietly, the second one of being less reliant on words, and the third step of moving my thoughts from making "to do" lists to focusing on spiritual questions and themes where God was working with me. But now I was being challenged to move to a fourth level of making room, that of stilling even my theological questions and thoughts, so as to present my mind and heart fully to God in the silence.[47]

In *An Interpretation of Friends Worship*, N. Jean Toomer, an African American pioneer of the Harlem Renaissance, acknowledges how difficult it is to turn within. He suggests that the first step is take an alert, upright, but relaxed position. When the body has become quiet, then one can seek to "still the mind, gather it, turn it steadfastly towards God."[48] He acknowledges that this is difficult because "it is contrary to the mind's nature to be still. It is against its grain to turn Godwards. Left to itself it goes on and on under its own momentum, roaming, wandering."[49] Because of the mind's "incessant restlessness," repeated effort and daily practice are necessary over the course of a lifetime.

Toomer writes that when joining with other Friends in a meeting for worship, he centers down and tries to open himself to God's Light and to the other people present. His intention is to become "just a little less conformed to the unregenerate ways of the world, just a little more conformed to the dedicated way of love."[50] He encourages a bold but humble expectation that "here, in this very meeting, before it is over, the Lord's power will spring up in us, cover the meeting, gather us to Him and to one another."[51] Even if nothing spectacular happens, he hopes to participate in an act of true prayer and worship. After focusing his intention and expectation, he waits:

I wait before the Lord, forgetting the words in which I clothed my expectations, if possible forgetting myself and my desires, laying down my will, asking only that His will be done. In attitude or silent words I may say, "I am before thee, Lord. If it be thy will, work thy love in me, work thy love in us." . . . Sometimes, while waiting, a glow steals over me, a warmth spreads from my heart. I have a chance to welcome the welling up of reverence, the sense that I am in the presence of the sacred. Sometimes, though rarely, the practice of waiting is invaded by an unexpected series of inner events which carry me by their action through the meeting to the end. I feel God's spirit moving in me, my spirit awakening to Him. Hardly a meeting passes but what I pray that I and the members of the meeting and people everywhere may have this experience: that our wills be overcome by God's will, that our powers be overpowered by His light and love and wisdom. And sometimes, though again rarely, I find it possible to hold my attention, or, rather, to have my heart held, without wavering, upon the one supreme reality, the sheer fact of God. These are the moments I feel to be true worship. These are the times when the effort to have faith is superseded by an effortless assurance born of actual experience. God's reality is felt in every fibre of the soul and brings convincement even to the body-mind.[52]

For Friends in the past and today, frequent practice in turning within, along with patient, repeated expectation of God's Presence, eventually leads to the kinds of experience that bring convincement, which is the subject of the next section of this book.

Reflection Questions

Turning Within

What has moved you to look more deeply into your own awareness?

Were there particular moments when you first sensed something divine within you or received divine guidance?

Have you always been aware of the indwelling divine Presence?

At present, when or how do you turn inward?

What makes it difficult to be still and look within?

What helps you to be patient or to "wait expectantly" when turning your attention to the inner dimensions of life?

Convincement

Turning inward, early Friends discovered the divine Light, the Spirit of Christ, dwelling within. They found God's law written on their hearts and received revelations or "openings" of what they called Truth: direct understanding of spiritual reality. Their community experienced manifestations of God's Presence within and among them. Both individually and as a group, they received divine guidance to change their lives in very specific ways.

As the indwelling Presence of Christ became evident, early Friends also became sharply aware—both in themselves and in their society—of sin, darkness, and "the world's ways, words, fashions, and customs."[53] With sometimes searing intensity, the inward Light revealed how thoroughly each person had been under the influence of spiritually oppressive forces. However much a person may have talked about God and engaged in religious practices, his or her actions had been primarily under the control of the human will, in conformity to social norms. Even those who had avoided most sinful behavior found that they had been inwardly bound or chained in ways they barely suspected. They were shocked to see how they had colluded with hypocrisy and the spiritual oppression of themselves and others. This way of living to which they had previously conformed was now viewed as a form of death.

Like the hard husk around a seed, the old self that was living in spiritual darkness needed to break open and disintegrate. A death of the old self was necessary in order for the seed—the Light of Christ Within—to take root and grow. The process of being turned from darkness to light is a process of being brought through death to rebirth. The disintegration of the old, willful self makes way for the birth of a new self that will reveal the divine image. There are three aspects to the process of turning to the Light: Openings, the Refiner's Fire, and Community. For the early

Quakers, all of these elements were part of the process of becoming a convinced Friend. More than that, they were necessary aspects of the transformation leading to rebirth as a child of the Light, a son or daughter of God.

Openings in the Seventeenth Century

> *I will put my law within them, and I will write it on their hearts; and I will be their God, and they shall be my people. No longer shall they teach one another, or say to each other, 'Know the Lord,' for they shall all know me, from the least of them to the greatest, says the Lord.*
>
> —Jeremiah 31:33–34

Early Quaker Isaac Penington wrote about how earthly "wisdom" and self-centered reasoning harden the human heart and conscience. However, when people start giving attention to the presence of the divine Light within, God makes people become

> *gentle and tender, fit to receive the impressions of his Spirit. By the influence and power of his Spirit on the conscience, he openeth the ear to hearken to his voice, and prepareth the heart to follow him in his leadings.*[54]

Penington advised a seeker to wait for "the opening of the eye of God in thee, and for the sight of things therewith, as they are from him."[55]

When people rest their attention on God within, the heart softens and the mind becomes quiet. Those who become receptive in this way experience flashes of direct knowing, revelations of divine Truth. For many of the first Quakers, revelations took the form of "openings in Scripture," in which the meaning of a particular Bible passage was revealed by the Holy Spirit in a way that spoke to each person's particular life situation and experience. Sometimes words of Scripture were heard inwardly, with authority, and were experienced as the voice of God speaking directly to the hearer.

In the 1640s, after finishing his apprenticeship as a weaver, William Dewsbury joined the Parliament's army, eager to fight for God's kingdom to be established in England. He was willing to give his life for it, if necessary. As a soldier, with his sword belted to his side, he walked to Scotland to visit Presbyterians who had a reputation for being zealous. Nowhere, however, did he find people who could tell him how God had freed them from sin. Finally, he began to seek God within. After a time of waiting, he had a powerful opening in the form of words from Scripture. When Peter sliced off the ear of the high priest's slave, Jesus told his disciple to put his sword away (Matthew 26:52–53). In John 18:36 (KJV), Jesus said to Pontius Pilate, *"My kingdom is not of this world: if my kingdom were of this world, then would my servants fight."*

One day Dewsbury inwardly heard these words with piercing power, as though spoken directly to him. This had a transforming effect:

> *Which word enlightened my heart, and discovered the mystery of iniquity; it showed the* kingdom of Christ to be within, *and that its enemies being within and spiritual, my weapons against them should be spiritual—the power of God.*[56]

Obeying Christ's command, Dewsbury got rid of his sword and quit the Army. Over time, he learned that God wanted him to fight to bring the divine kingdom to earth using spiritual weapons: truth, love, forgiveness, sacrifice, and long-suffering.

Wholehearted seekers all over England experienced openings that transformed their understanding. Not all openings were conveyed through the words of Scripture. After giving up hope that any priest or preacher would be able to guide his soul, George Fox discovered that guidance was available from within:

> When all my hopes in them and in all men were gone, so that I had nothing outwardly to help me, nor could tell what to do, then, oh then, I heard a voice which said, "There is one, even Christ Jesus, that can speak to thy condition", and when I heard it, my heart did leap for joy.[57]

In Yorkshire, Richard Farnsworth had a similar opening. For years he had attended sermons, sought guidance from priests, prayed zealously, and memorized Scripture. This had not released him from his burden of sin, so he began to stay home alone on Sundays, waiting for God's revelation. One day he heard the inward voice of Christ, which said, "I will teach thee freely myself, and all the children of the Lord shall be taught of the Lord, and in righteousness shall they be established."[58] Farnsworth began corresponding with Fox. Soon they were traveling together to share the good news of the teaching that comes directly from the inward Christ.

Some openings come in the form of images or visions. While traveling in Yorkshire with Farnsworth, Fox felt moved to climb to the top of Pendle Hill. On the windy summit, he had a panoramic view of the countryside. He also saw something with his spiritual eyes: "And the Lord let me see a-top of the hill in what places he had a great people to be gathered." At the nearby inn where the two men stayed that night, Fox had a further vision in which he saw people wearing white, "by a river's side coming to the Lord."[59] He therefore walked north, into parts of England near the Rawthey and Lune rivers. There he encountered numerous groups of Seekers who had been waiting for a prophet to show them how God wanted them to worship.

On Pentecost Sunday—a day when people traditionally wore white—Fox preached powerfully to a large group of Separatists at Justice Benson's home. The group encouraged him to speak the following Sunday at Firbank

Fell; there, a thousand Seekers heard him speak. Hundreds were immediately "opened" to the Truth in Fox's message, and they were quickly gathered into a new movement, the radical form of Christianity soon called Quakerism.

The first openings of most early Friends revealed that God's ways are different from the ways of the world. In particular, Friends sensed Christ asking them to change how they spoke, dressed, and participated in the flattering mores of society, all of which supported a class system that denied people's inherent spiritual equality. For poor rural people who already lived a simple life, plainness was not as difficult as it was for the rich and well-established. Lady Mary Springett had married Isaac Penington, a Cambridge-educated theologian and son of a former Lord Mayor of London. They scorned the first Quakers they met, common country people from the north of England, less educated and less refined than themselves. Nonetheless, certain things they heard the Quakers say made them wonder if these rough people might be speaking the truth. In her journal, Mary Penington wrote,

> *Immediately it arose in my mind, that if I would know whether that was truth they had spoken or not, I must do what I knew to be the Lord's will. What was contrary to it was now set before me, as to be removed; and I must come into a state of entire obedience, before I could be in a capacity to perceive or discover what it was which they laid down for their principles.*[60]

She was seeking intellectual understanding, but this first opening revealed that what God desired before all else was a change in her way of life.

Early Friends spoke often of a divine Power they felt during their gatherings, when many had a transforming awareness of the presence of Christ in their midst. In 1658, Isaac Penington felt his first unmistakable opening while attending a large gathering held on a country estate. Knowing that accepting the Quaker message would radically

43

change his life, Penington prayed intently beforehand that he might accept God's Truth, and only God's Truth:

> *I went with fear and trembling, with desires to the Most High, who was over all, and knew all, that I might not receive any thing for truth which was not of him, nor withstand any thing which was of him; but might bow before the appearance of the Lord my God, and none other.*[61]

In a state of humble, sincere openness, together with thousands of Friends, Penington entered into worship to wait upon God's Spirit. In the silence he "felt the presence and power of the Most High."[62]

Then George Fox stood and explained that Christ was within as a divine Seed. Penington felt "words of truth from the Spirit of truth reaching to my heart and conscience, opening up my state as in the presence of the Lord."[63] He was finally able to distinguish clearly between the willful mental state from which all his intellectual, theological analysis had previously come and a sensitive, holy, inward Presence that was beyond the power of his intellect to control. Penington had subtly sensed this before but had not thought it worthy of attention. Society and his education had trained him to have contempt for the humble, simple, *feeling* way that Christ had always been present within. Like others, he had been expecting a glorious outward Second Coming of Christ visible to everyone and universally acknowledged. Looking for a powerful king mounted on a strong horse, he had overlooked the baby in the manger, the small divine Seed in his own heart. His heart broke open and Penington recognized his savior within. He wrote,

> *This is he, there is no other; this is he whom I have waited for and sought after from my childhood; who was always near me, and had often begotten life in my heart; but I knew him not distinctly, nor how to receive him, or dwell with him.*[64]

Early Friends turned to God not only during special daily periods of prayer and devotion but at various moments throughout the day. They found that intimacy with God was possible while walking outdoors and even while lying in their beds at night. Most participated at least twice a week in meetings for worship that lasted for several hours. During periods of complete silence, they were made intimately aware of the basic mental processes that distract attention away from God, including "vain thoughts, imaginings, and wanderings of the mind." They learned to observe and then let go of these distracting mental activities, turning their attention again and again to the Light within. The focus of the gathered group was a great aid to each person in becoming free of the grip of their own thinking, allowing their individual self to be "crucified" so that they could open to the mind of God. The direct presence and guidance of the Spirit of Christ—the Light—helped them collectively to move beyond ordinary human mental constraints. Although discipline and surrender were necessary, early Friends did not believe it was by their own power that transformation happened. The power came from God.

As a young man from a wealthy family, Thomas Ellwood knew that taking up Quaker ways would displease his father and his friends, so he felt troubled by his attraction to Quakerism. Nonetheless, after attending one meeting for worship, he felt he needed to attend another. During the second one, he experienced a powerful sense of opening, a clearing of the confusion that had clouded him:

> *My understanding began to open, and I felt some stirrings in my breast, tending to the work of a new creation in me. The general trouble and confusion of mind, which had for some days lain heavy upon me and pressed me down, without a distinct discovery of the particular cause for which it came, began to wear off, and some glimmerings of light began to break forth in me, which let me see my inward state and condition towards God.*[65]

45

At a subsequent meeting, Ellwood received further openings:

Edward Burrough's ministry came forth among us in life and power, and the assembly was covered therewith. . . . I felt some of that divine power working my spirit into a great tenderness, and not only confirming me in the course I had already entered, and strengthening me to go on therein, but rending also the veil somewhat further, and clearing my understanding in some other things which I had not seen before.[66]

As Quaker converts opened to the inward Light and embraced God's desire for them to take up a more simple, honest way of life, some were inspired with great enthusiasm or had ecstatic experiences. This happened frequently in the first ten or fifteen years of the Quaker movement. Some experienced the quaking that earned early Friends their nickname, Quakers. The first time Margaret Fell told her husband, Thomas Fell, about the message of George Fox, she and her whole family were startled by how she trembled while sitting at the dinner table.[67] Others quaked in public while speaking to judges in the courtroom or crowds in the marketplace.

Some were opened to the reality of God's active presence by witnessing miracles. George Fox reported that several miraculous healings occurred at the home of Elizabeth Hooton. The first took place during a meeting for worship of the Children of Light, when a woman was healed who had been so mentally disturbed, and for so long, that she was considered to be possessed. William Dewsbury witnessed several "signs and wonders" while traveling with George Fox and Richard Hubberthorne, including the healing of a woman who had been lame. Bent over and hobbling on crutches, she was enabled to stand straight and walk without assistance. Dewsbury took this and other occurrences as signs that God was truly inspiring the new Quaker movement. He had been fervently praying for such confirmation.[68] Fox's prayer and touch was connected with the healing of numerous physical conditions, even the full restoration of health to some who were close to death. He compiled a *Book of Miracles* containing accounts of more than one hundred miracles that had occurred in his presence.[*] Quakers of a later generation were uncomfortable with the charismatic experiences of the first Friends, and many of the references to healings and prophetic dreams were removed when the *Journal of George Fox* was first published.

Openings come in many forms. Sometimes the illumination of the Light provides a profound experience of divine Love or Presence or gives inward power to overcome wrong behaviors, bad habits, and temptations. Openings are sometimes accompanied by courageous strength to speak or act in faithful and prophetic ways. Those who are discouraged are opened to hope. Some openings are dramatic and involve physical manifestations, but most involve subtle perceptions that come after quieting the mind and waiting patiently for the indwelling Presence or Light to reveal itself. Many openings come as a quietly growing conviction about how God wants one to believe, speak, and act, along with a growing ability to live a righteous, faithful, and holy life.

Not every thought, image, feeling, or line of Scripture that comes into one's mind is fresh guidance from God. In the process of opening to divine instruction, each person gradually learns to distinguish the inward "voice of the true shepherd" from other kinds of inner "voices," including the promptings of temptations and desire or remembered advice and admonishment given by other people. Growth in the spiritual life involves an increasingly refined ability to discern the source of the thoughts, ideas, feelings, and impulses that come into one's mind and heart, to know which ones carry spiritual truth and guidance from God

---

[*] The manuscript of the *Book of Miracles* has disappeared, although the index for it remains. It has been partially reconstructed by Harvard scholar Henry J. Cadbury.

and Christ and which do not. The discernment of the community is a helpful and sometimes necessary aid.

The insights, guidance, revelations, and manifestations of God's Power that have been described as openings here are the sort of experiences that are generally welcomed by the receiver. However, when early Quakers turned within, they also experienced the Light showing them things that were hard to see. For example, they were shown that behavior that had seemed to be harmless social conformity was contrary to God's ways. Richard Farnsworth wrote,

> In waiting upon the Lord, in the light of the Spirit of truth I found much inward peace, joy, comfort, and satisfaction to my soul, and the righteous law of the spirit of life set up within, convincing of sin.[69]

Thomas Ellwood explained that the difficult revelations were presented to him gradually,

> For the Lord was pleased to make His discoveries to me by degrees, that the sight of too great a work, and too many enemies to encounter with at once, might not discourage me and make me faint.[70]

These kinds of openings are part of the element of the spiritual journey called the Refiner's Fire.

Openings in Our Time

God is speaking to people today as much as ever, revealing truth and showing the way. As at the beginning of Quakerism, the most fundamental kind of opening reveals the divine Presence within people and active in the world. Most openings reveal God's Wisdom and Love. Some contain divine guidance about how to live in accordance with God's will. What is revealed is beyond words. Most Friends today use the words *God* or *Christ* to speak of what they encounter. Some Friends, however, use other words, or metaphors, such as Spirit, the Light, the Holy One, Presence, or divine Mystery.

Children are often aware of the divine presence, although they may not identify that presence as God. For example, as a child Margaret Hope Bacon experienced

> *moments which I now regard as openings; feelings of intense identification with the whole of creation, of the expansion of self into the universe as I looked up into the heavens on a starry night. I had no concept of God onto which to hang these feelings; they seemed to have no relation to the stern old man with a beard whom my mother had rejected. Rather the spirit I felt at these moments was warm, nurturing, growthful, motherlike. The universe was on my side, I dimly felt. The ocean, in which I loved to dive and swim, would sustain me, bear me up, heal me of any hurt, carry me safe toward shore.*[71]

The first major opening sometimes comes out of the blue. However, it usually follows a period of seeking for meaning or spiritual understanding. Ben Pink Dandelion, a British professor of Quaker studies, was an atheist at the time he took a research trip to the United States and traveled by bus from the East Coast to San Francisco and back. On his return trip, in danger of missing his flight home, he spent every cent he had to get a ticket on another bus line. With no money left for food, he fasted. On the bus he became aware for the first time of the presence of God:

> *In the midst of this onward journey, just outside St. Louis, unbidden, unwanted, unimagined, and all the more powerful and compelling for all that, I felt lifted up and cradled by what I have called God, held and reassured. . . . It was a powerful experience for me and, delightfully, has never left me. Since that time, I have lived an accompanied life. The most amazing things have happened and synchronicity abounds. God is with me, and I know this, in George Fox's terms, experientially.*[72]

For many, the first major opening is associated with a decision to offer oneself to God and surrender willful control. After a period of listening daily for "the still small voice within," Louise Wilson sensed that she needed to relinquish her willfulness:

> *One morning I knew I could not hold on to my will, and pray[ed] that God's will would be done in and through me. The contradiction I felt from within seemed to push me to the place where I handed my will over to God, literally. What rejoicing! I heard the music of the universe and I was in harmony with the music. I wanted to continually give over my will. That was my prayer. That moment was the beginning of what became my intentional spiritual journey.*[73]

Recorded Friends minister* Peggy Senger Morrison had a life-transforming opening in college that also involved surrender. At age twelve she had rebelled against religion because many Christians she knew were hypocritical, and some were overtly racist. It seemed to her that God was passive in the face of many evils. At the liberal arts college she attended, students read classic texts, asking if they were true and, if so, how that truth would change their lives. During her freshman year, she read Sophocles, Archimedes, and Plato. The next year, students read the Bible cover to cover under the guidance of two quirky, world-renowned scholars, one a Jew and the other a Russian Orthodox bishop. This helped Morrison get in touch with truth:

> *And I found that the truth wasn't in the book, or in other people—glowing or not—and it wasn't in the discussion or the dogma or the reading, it was inside me and I recognized it and began to live. I walked out of the seminar hall into the*

---

* Some branches of Quakerism record the gifts of ministry of members of their meetings.

foothills of the Sangre de Cristo Mountains and I looked at the sky and I said:

"I know you are there/here. I know you want me/have me. I surrender."

And nothing changed and everything changed. But a conversation started that night that has never really stopped. I accepted Life on Life's terms. God is God. The deal is what it is. Huge pieces of the deal hurt. A lot of the people are unmitigated screw-ups, including me. But I am awake, alive, connected, real. I fake less. I am scared less. And I have to surrender every day.[74]

In the midst of a time of physical pain and confusion, when he was praying nightly for God's help, Bolivian Raúl Choque Mamani experienced a remarkable, life-changing opening after weeks of speaking to God each night. One evening, feeling a painful hardness in his heart, he repeated over and over, "I don't know if God exists and, if you exist, help me." Something began to shift inside.

I felt a kind of light rain inside me, as though something were wetting me. Then I continued praying and after a while had passed, I felt even more breaking of my heart and the presence of the Lord. That is to say, my poor steel heart was melting! The doubts and illness had begun to disappear from my life. How beautiful that moment was! Thanks to the Lord I say even today in tears![75]

He was healed of the troubling pain in the back of his neck. As in this case, openings are often associated with a sensation of an interior softening of some part of the body, often the heart area.

Many openings contain a call upon one's life. Wilmer Cooper was raised among the most plain of the Conservative Friends in Ohio, nurtured by his family, community, and Quaker boarding school. His family disapproved of higher education, but he longed for something more. After high school, he started working for his relatives but felt something beckoning him. One Sunday afternoon in winter, while meditating and praying in his family's warm greenhouse, he received direction for his life:

> *Suddenly, I had a very strong sense of call that I was to go to college the next year and that I was to prepare for some important work and service ahead.*[76]

Later, he looked upon what happened in the greenhouse as *a religious experience involving a conversion. My life turned from where it had been going to a much more intentional life, undergirded with a sense of direction and divine purpose.*[77]

In a life increasingly centered on God, each person gradually opens to more and more spiritual understanding. For those who are attentive and focused on God, direct revelations of divine Truth and guidance can become a frequent experience. Some openings contain guidance for the moment or for a lifetime. Other openings are part of an ongoing revelation of divine Reality. In her journal, Quaker teacher Sandra Cronk describes an opening she received while attending meeting for worship when she was thirty-two years old. She was pondering "the new creation" described in Romans 8:21–22.

> *I kept wondering what this new creation would be like. . . . Why can't I see it or feel it? Then in the meeting this morning, I did feel it. I wanted to express it in words for all present. I could not articulate it. I decided it did not need to be said. All could experience it. It was the experience of that Being out of which all our doing should come. It is that Being toward which so much of our doing strives frantically but never reaches because the Being is already there and we do not know it.*[78]

Before becoming a Quaker, Helene Pollock attended seminary and worked as clergy. She had been a committed Christian all of her life. Then one day, seemingly out of the blue, a profound shift in her consciousness took place, and she encountered divine Love:

Suddenly, without warning, one night I was beset by the profound sense that my whole universe had changed in a delicious sort of way. The horizon rose to meet the sky, and I found myself rising into the infinity of the stars. I was infused by the heart of the universe, while remaining very much on the ground. It was as if the stars were reaching out and calling my name—as if I were united with the vastness of all the grains of sand on all the beaches that ever were, yet I remained as small and insignificant as the tiniest grain of sand. This sense of dislocation in time and space was accompanied by an overwhelming sensation of joy, along with a feeling of being loved by Love itself, and thereby in love with everyone and everything. The Christian Gospel that I had known all my life came to me with fresh intensity. The experience was so very personal that I knew that God had reached out to me alone—touching my heart in the precise way that I, Helene, most needed to be reached. I experienced myself being newly christened into the Christian story of a God who takes on personal, human form in the incarnation of Jesus, the enfleshed embodiment of Divine Love.[79]

After this experience, God became the focus of Pollock's life in a much fuller way. Some of the most profoundly transforming openings, like Pollock's, involve a direct encounter with God's Love.

Many openings reveal God's presence and activity in the world in new ways. After attending a Quaker meeting for a while, Deborah Saunders was opened to God's universality:

Gradually I began to understand what Friends meant by God being present in every person, not only people within the Religious Society of Friends, but people universally. I saw God in the homeless person, in the drug addict, in my brothers and sisters who differed from me in their sexual orientation, in their mental or physical capabilities, even in those whose religious views differed significantly from mine. I saw humanity as I saw myself—all of us made in the image and likeness of the Divine.[80]

Openings reveal both how God wants us to live and how we are failing to do so. Each person's inner condition is closely connected with the fears and denials that are part of that person's culture. Injuries and limited beliefs are passed down from generation to generation. In our time, we are opened to see the ways that our society and social structures are not in keeping with God's Love and Truth. Those who repeatedly turn to the divine Presence within are made increasingly sensitive to deception, oppression, and injustice in behaviors that had previously been seen as normal and unchangeable. It's easy to look back and identify mistaken beliefs and harmful behaviors of previous centuries. It's harder and riskier to identify the illusions and underlying systems of oppression and destruction in our own day. God opens us to insights and unsettling experiences that show us how our society is out of balance and how we participate in behaviors that are unjust or destructive to the earth.

Elizabeth Gordon had an opening in an especially deep meeting for worship in New Paltz, New York, that showed her how her nation had turned away from divine guidance again and again regarding race relations:

Twenty or so silent people on plain wooden benches facing the unornamented center of a plain room. The silence ran unbroken for a time, and then deepened suddenly, as a stream opening into a deep pool. Sitting within this silence, I seemed to drift into a sort of movie, more conceptual than visual, but I felt I could see the concepts in a way. They were outlined against a patina of sadness, a sadness that seemed to be around me but not in me, at first. What I saw was American history as a series of missed opportunities to right the wrong of slavery.[81]

The images started with the advent of chattel slavery in North American through the Civil War, revealing missed opportunities afterwards to right the systemic wrongs done to Africans and African Americans and continuing until the present day. Gordon began quaking and rose to offer vocal ministry to the meeting. Afterwards, a heartfelt prayer came:

Sitting, eyes closed, I had prayed then as one washed ashore. Let me do something, let no new harm be done, let the wounds be healed, let us not miss the next opportunity. Use me. Change me. Use me.[82]

The vision and the prayer shaped Gordon's life in the years to come.

Openings not only reveal what is wrong in the world but provide guidance about how to live in accordance with God's will. When forced to decide whether or not to participate in war, many Quakers have powerful openings. Often young men who wrestle with the Quaker peace testimony finally experience within themselves the truth of Christ's call to a life of nonviolence. Usually this certainty does not come as an instantaneous revelation but as a result of a gradual process of listening for intimations of God's Truth and struggling with fears. After becoming a Quaker, educator Paul Lacey wondered if he could make a commitment to nonviolence:

The issue came to focus when I was trying to determine whether I could call myself a conscientious objector, recognizing that such a

step would mean foreswearing violence for the
rest of my life. For weeks I felt haunted by the
question, torn by my unfaithfulness if I did not
accept the peace testimony and terrified at its
irrationality and danger, if I did. This long
period of constant worry culminated in one
sleepless night which I spent arguing with
myself, going over the arguments of others,
praying for guidance and being afraid that I
might have my prayers answered. Finally, early
in the morning, I knew I had crossed the line. No
new arguments fell into place, nothing became
more rational, but somewhere I had changed and
I knew that I would have to declare myself a
conscientious objector and give up reliance on
force to accomplish things—for the rest of my
life.[83]

The decision put Lacey at odds with some members of his family. He was worried that he might have to go to prison for his pacifism and even more frightened that his commitment to nonviolence would lessen his safety in the world: "Suddenly I was utterly defenseless in a violent world, and for a long time I went through my days fearful of what it meant to have disarmed myself."[84] Life provided him opportunities to work with his fear, however, and when he was later faced with dangerous situations, he did not resort to violent self-defense.

Openings do not always happen during quiet moments in solitude or worship. Sometimes they occur in the midst of action in the world. When Occupy Wall Street protests began in New York City's financial district in September 2011, Micah Bales felt the Holy Spirit urging him to travel north and participate. He had been disillusioned by experiences as an activist in college, and as a seminary student, he had focused on how to nurture the inward spiritual life of others. However, while marching through the streets of lower Manhattan and down Wall Street, he was struck by the traces of opulent luxury he saw along the way and the contrast between the most wealthy and the working class. The experience opened Bales to see more clearly "how the abusive power of the corporations and big banks dominate our society and mock our democratic process."[85] He felt called to participate in a movement that questioned the "concentration of power in the hands of the few."[86] He returned home to Washington, D.C., and helped to organize Occupy DC in McPherson Square.

Openings that show us how the ways of the world are not in harmony with God's desires for justice, love, and peace often lead us into the next elements of the spiritual journey.

Reflection Questions

Openings

Have you ever experienced openings, revelations, spiritual insights, guidance, intuitions, or consolations from God, Christ, the Holy Spirit, or the inward Teacher?

How have you come to understand what God wants of you, your community, or of humanity? Have any "openings in Scripture" shifted your understanding of what God wants?

Have you had a deeper *seeing* of what the world is like now and what it could be?

Have you found it difficult to accept and remember the openings you have experienced? When and to whom have you talked about your experience of openings?

The Refiner's Fire in the Seventeenth Century

*The Lord whom you seek will suddenly come to his
temple. . . . But who can endure the day of his
coming, and who can stand when he appears? For
he is like a refiner's fire and like fullers' soap.*

—Malachi 3:1b, 2

For early Friends the initial experience of the Light was
often very challenging, sometimes even terrifying, for the
penetrating Light revealed everything that was resistant or
contrary to God's Love and Truth. When introducing their
faith to others, early Quakers told people how to discover
the Light of Christ within. Look into your conscience, they
counseled. Pay attention to whatever makes your
conscience uneasy, and the Light will illuminate how you
resist God. For many, it was a surprise to discover
uncontrolled desires, deceitful manners, unjust social
practices, greed, pride, and fear within themselves. Early
Friends spoke of "temptations," "the pollutions of the
world," or "the wiles of Satan." At the beginning of the
Quaker movement, seeing and accepting how thoroughly
one had been under the sway of negative influences was
foundational to becoming a Friend. The early Quakers
became acutely aware of the ways they had learned, along
with the rest of their society, to ignore, deny, and suppress
the inward experience of the divine Presence. As traveling
Quaker ministers Katharine Evans and Sarah Chevers,
while imprisoned in Malta, told the Inquisitors, "We were
children of wrath once as well as others."[87]

Not long after George Fox opened to the guidance of the
inward Christ, he began to experience the Refiner's Fire:

> *But oh, then did I see my troubles, trials, and
> temptations more than ever I had done! As the
> light appeared, all appeared that is out of the
> light, darkness, death, temptations, the unright-
> eous, the ungodly; all was manifest and seen in*

59

the Light. Then after this there did appear a pure fire in me; then I saw how he sat as at a refiner's fire and as the fuller's soap; and then the spiritual discerning came into me, by which I did discern my own thoughts, groans and sighs, and what it was that did veil me, and what it was that did open me. And that which could not abide in the patience nor endure the fire, in the Light I found to be the groans of the flesh (that could not give up to the will of God), which had veiled me, and that could not be patient in all trials, troubles and anguishes and perplexities, and could not give up self to die by the Cross.[88]

The Light shows these things not primarily in order to condemn people but to reveal truth and to bring about change. Nonetheless, this kind of revelation is painful. As the prophet Malachi warned, the God who appears among the people (or in this case *within* the people) is intent upon purification, like a fuller or a refiner. A fuller's job is to scrub the dirty, rough wool of a sheep until it is clean and soft, ready to be spun and woven into cloth. A refiner purifies a lump of silver or gold by putting it into a hot fire to melt away all the base metals within until it becomes pure. The more precious the metal, the hotter the fire needed for this refining process.

In an epistle to Friends at large, Margaret Fell urged Friends to

let the living Principle of God in you all, examine what ye enjoy and possess of him, who is Eternal; and what is of him, will stand in his Presence, which is a Consuming Fire to all that is not of him.[89]

In the seventeenth century, the prospect of eternal damnation was vivid in people's minds and conviction of one's sins was especially frightening. Nonetheless, seeing how they had been erring from divine Truth and Love ultimately brought people closer to God. Richard

Hubberthorne had an intense experience of the Refiner's Fire soon after coming to Quakerism. He wrote to George Fox to say that "the hand of the Lord hath been mightily exercised on me."[90] The power of God, he wrote, "caused a flame to enter within me, to destroy the lust which had fed upon stolen waters and bread gotten by deceit; for I have fed upon vanity and lies."[91] Sarah Blackborow urged people to accept such revelations: "Oh! love truth and its Testimony, whether its Witness be to you, or against you, love it."[92]

Most early Friends were surprised to discover in themselves the "seeds" of all the evils of which human beings are capable. Although they did not have the language of psychology to describe what the Light revealed about their condition, they had a sophisticated understanding of their inner workings. They described human tendencies with reference to biblical characters, including Cain and Esau. The Light reveals a divided self, torn between different kinds of motivations. Fox, for example, discovered competing "thirsts" inside himself. The thirst for creature comforts and social status competed with the thirst to unite fully with God's will. Early Quakers spoke of two kinds of inner "seeds" that were in competition with each other. The "wicked" or "contrary" seed (sometimes called the "serpent's seed") loved comfort and conformity to the ways of the world; this was in competition with the divine "immortal" Seed, the Seed of Christ, that longed to change the ways of the world and bring about the kingdom of heaven on earth. They saw their condition within the context of a larger cosmic battle and viewed their lives as part of the human-divine story described in the Bible.

In the Refiner's Fire one becomes acutely aware of the inward struggle. Painfully, one notices those occasions when the desires of the flesh and the cravings for social acceptance dominate, squelching the inward promptings of the Spirit. If allowed to grow, the serpent's seed becomes a weed that chokes out the divine Seed. However, with diligence and surrender to God, the divine Seed grows and takes dominion. Understanding this was key to the Quaker spiritual experience. Isaac Penington wrote,

> *This is the sum or substance of our religion; to wit, to feel and discern the two seeds: the seed of enmity, the seed of love; the seed of the flesh, the seed of the Spirit . . . and to feel the judgments of God administered to the one of these, till it be brought into bondage and death; and the other raised up in the love and mercy of the Lord to live in us, and our souls gathered into it, to live to God in it.*[93]

Early Quaker tract writer William Smith described how each person must be "in his own Conscience convinced of the things that are evil."[94] In seventeenth-century England, *convinced* meant *proven guilty*. It was a term used in the courtroom, similar to "convicted." A person became a convinced Quaker after being shown the errors of his or her ways, admitting them, surrendering to God's judgment, and becoming liberated for a new kind of life. The Light reveals all the internal thoughts, mental patterns, and fantasies that resist the work of God. Although it is painful to see one's internal conflict, continuing to face the Light and to see what it reveals in one's own mind, heart, and behavior allows God to refine, or melt away, the inner impediments to the Light. During the course of the spiritual journey, Friends were put through numerous "spiritual exercises" in the process of purification. God's ways gradually overcome the tendency to be dominated by the ways of the world and the baser human instincts.

Religious life is not just about holding particular beliefs about God and Christ or praying or worshiping properly on the Sabbath. Every aspect of life has a spiritual significance. The people of England had highly mannered, class-conscious ways of speaking, dressing, and greeting others, behaviors all designed to indicate in every interaction whose social status was higher and whose was lower. Seventeenth-century English Quakers recognized they had been participating in numerous outward behaviors that denied the spiritual equality of all, behavior that they now saw as contrary to God's will. Honor was due to God, not to human beings. Therefore, doffing one's hat, or bowing, or addressing a single person in plural form were all acts of deceit. Revealed by the Light, each act of deceitfulness and conformity to oppressive social practices, however common, was felt keenly as a betrayal of divine Truth. Early Friends experienced God requiring them to stop dressing, talking, and behaving in ostentatious and untruthful ways, even though their nonconformity made them peculiar to others.

The requirement to change plunges people deeper into the Refiner's Fire. In many ways, it is more comfortable to conform to society than to model a different way of life. The physical body, too, though sacred, wants to indulge the desires of the flesh, and it groans at the arduous requirements of the soul. After being freed from a difficult imprisonment, Elizabeth Hooton was "exercised" by an inner struggle about risking arrest again. Gradually, she learned to discern the voice of Christ and distinguish it from the comfort-loving reasoning process she described as "Satan's wiles." Gifted Quaker speaker James Nayler underwent a mighty struggle between the divine call to travel in the ministry and the natural human desire to stay at home with his family; his conflict led to serious illness, and he was at the brink of death before he was ready to follow God's call.

Early Quakers used many names and images for the Refiner's Fire. It was called "the saving baptism of the spirit" and a "washing." It was the pruning necessary to make a tree more fruitful and the "axe at the root" of any tree that did not produce good fruit. It was a stripping that left one naked before God. They spoke of the hammer and the sword of the Lord. Whether by inner baptism, rough scrubbing, pruning, stripping, or through the heat of the Refiner's Fire, this merciful "ministration" was a process of purification and regeneration leading to life as a new kind of person.

The Refiner's Fire continued for years and decades, purifying mind and heart until every distraction and sinful tendency was removed. Eventually, the pristine original divine nature of humanity was restored, making possible the full growth of the inner divine Seed. This refining process is a prelude to spiritual rebirth, the birth of Christ within. "In the Refining Fire," Smith explains, every form of corruption

> is purged and consumed; and as Man abides the Fire, and waits in the Judgment, he puts off the Old in which he hath lived, and he puts on the New and is translated; and here man truly dies to himself, and receives Christ the Seed of Life, and putteth him on.[95]

After hearing George Fox speak on Firbank Fell, Francis Howgill was immediately convinced of the truth of what he heard; it resonated with his inward experience and decades of longing and seeking. Along with hundreds of others that day, he was convinced he'd been looking for God in the wrong ways and following a spirit that was not divine: "We were all seen to be off the foundation, and all mouths were stopped in the dust. We all stood as condemned in ourselves, and all saw our nakedness, and were all ashamed."[96] Biblical images, many from the Book of Revelation, came to Howgill's mind to give meaning to the experience that afterward consumed him for months and utterly transformed his life:

> My eyes were opened, and all the things that I had ever done were brought to my remembrance and the ark of the testament was opened, and there was thunder and lightning and great hail. . . . And in the morning I wished it had been evening, and in the evening I wished it had been morning and I had no rest, but trouble on every side. And all that I had ever done was judged and condemned. . . . I

*became a perfect fool, and knew nothing, as a man
distracted; all was overturned, and I suffered loss
of all. In all that I ever did, I saw it was in the
accursed nature.* [97]

The turning point came when Howgill acknowledged the
truth of the divine judgment he felt inside:

*And then something in me cried: "Just and true is
his judgment!" . . . And as I did give up all to the
judgment, the captive came forth out of prison and
rejoiced, and my heart was filled with joy. I came
to see him whom I had pierced, and my heart was
broken. . . . Then I saw the cross of Christ, and
stood in it, and . . . a new man was made. And so
peace came to be made and so eternal life was
brought in through death and judgment. And then
the perfect gift I received, which was given from
God, and the holy law of God was revealed unto
me, and was written in my heart.* [98]

Like Francis Howgill, numerous early Friends had
intense and dramatic experiences. Most, however,
experienced a slower process. After John Banks first began
attending Quaker meetings, he became aware of the
purifying aspect of the Light of Christ Within:

*I [came] to be convinced by the living
appearance of the Lord Jesus of the evil and
vanity, sin and wickedness that the world lies in
(and that I was so much a partaker thereof.) . . .
But by taking true heed thereunto, through
watchfulness and fear, I came[,] by one little
after another[,] to be sensible of the work thereof
in my heart and soul, in order to subdue and
bring down, tame and subject the wild nature in
me, and to wash, purge, and cleanse me
inwardly from sin and corruption; for that end
that I might be changed and converted.* [99]

In 1668, after she had been a Quaker for about a decade, Mary Penington wrote of her ongoing experience of the Refiner's Fire. Her words indicate God's loving intention in revealing, day by day, her weaknesses and temptations:

> *Though various infirmities and temptations beset me, yet my heart cleaveth unto the Lord, in the everlasting bonds that can never be broken. In his light do I see those temptations and infirmities: there do I bemoan myself unto him, and feel faith and strength, which give the victory. Though it keeps me low in the sense of my own weakness, yet it quickens in me a lively hope of seeing Satan trodden down under foot by his all-sufficient grace. I feel and know when I have slipped in word, deed, or thought; and also know where my help lieth, who is my advocate, and have recourse to him who pardons and heals, and gives me to overcome, setting me on my watch-tower. . . . Oh! that I may, by discovering my own weakness, ever be tender of the tempted; watching and praying, lest I also be tempted. Sweet is this state, though low; for in it I receive my daily bread, and enjoy that which he handeth forth continually; and live not, but as he breatheth the breath of life upon me every moment.*[100]

The convincement experienced by early Friends made them aware of how they were not following God's ways. Although this was a painful experience that sometimes lasted an uncomfortably long time, ultimately it freed them to a new life. Unlike most of their contemporaries, they were henceforth not burdened by an ongoing sense of sinfulness. Rather, they were confident that they would be shown, step by step, how to overcome sin and become free.

The Refiner's Fire in Our Time

Experiences of the Light are challenging when they show us ways we have not been living in accordance with God's Love and Truth. Western cultures teach people from infancy onward to push divine guidance to the back of our awareness, and most people quickly learn to block perception of the indwelling Presence of God. Reversing this and consciously opening our hearts and minds to spiritual truth is not easy. It takes patience and courage to still our minds, turn within, and wait in a receptive way for the Light to show us how we have been resisting divine Love and Truth in the particulars of our thinking, our relationships, our way of living, and our participation in the world. Seeing this can be surprising. It is humbling to acknowledge the ways we have been deceiving both ourselves and others, and it is frightening to know the specific ways God wants us to stop conforming to society.

In our time, many Friends do not become aware of the refining aspect of the inward Light until they are well along in their spiritual journey. Nonetheless, opening to God's Presence and Love still initiates the difficult process of seeing and letting go of old ways. In *Dark Night's Journey*, Sandra Cronk writes,

> *The process of entering into a deep relationship with God is also the process of uncovering ourselves. Those places inside ourselves which we have hidden from the world, and even from our own consciousness, are now opened for God to reorder. Those deep hurts we had walled off for protection can finally be healed. The angers, fears, and lusts we had rationalized away are revealed for what they are. We can be transformed and healed by God's love. . . . In the light of that love, deep re-patterning can take place in us.*[101]

Eventually, flashes of insight and self-awareness become frequent for those who are paying inward attention. In a life lived in communion with God and Christ, within, there are daily opportunities to see how we fall short of love and truth in our thoughts, words, and actions. The Light reveals glimpses of how our inner wounds or insecurities motivate us to believe untruths and behave in ways that are false. Such glimpses happen in times of quiet introspection, prayer, or waiting on God. They also sometimes come in the midst of activity. Quaker sociologist Elise Boulding describes a moment when a sudden sense of the invisible presence of Jesus made her aware of the true motivations for her behavior. She writes,

> *I . . . was engaged in one of those verbal harangues on spiritual matters that we often use to cover our own emptiness. Suddenly he was there, silent and intent, and I heard and saw my babbling self. Quieting down quickly, I felt taught without words. He stayed with me for some days after that, and returns from time to time, though not often. He does not come in a time of crisis, but in times of spiritual barrenness.*[102]

It is often in the context of our interactions with others that God reveals the mistaken beliefs, inner wounds, and fears that veil the Light within us. Our most intimate relationships—with spouses, family members, coworkers, and community members—are opportunities for the Refiner's Fire to work in us in a daily way, slowly changing us over time if we attend to what is revealed within. In his autobiography *Drawn by the Light*, university professor Arthur O. Roberts writes candidly about how everything in his life served as a means for God to reach, teach, and change him, including parenting, being married, teaching, and serving as a pastor. One chapter tells that in many circumstances the Roberts children provided "a mirror," forcing the parents to examine their behavior in fresh ways.[103] Another chapter describes his experiments, as a young pastor, with his ability to sway people through use of his intellect and speaking gifts. God asked for his attention and "offered first personal assurance, then forthright judgment, and finally guidance."[104] Roberts received an important inward teaching,

> *There are better ways, God told the humbled servant, than manipulating people through rhetorical skill and applied psychology. Use your gift for words with integrity. Let wisdom, not cleverness, become your base . . . look at people with love, through the eyes of a compassionate Christ.*[105]

In a movingly honest chapter, Roberts describes how marriage also served as a crucible for the Refiner's Fire for both him and his wife, Fern. By midlife, after decades of experiencing burdens, disappointments, and deferred dreams, they had become distant from each other. His career and her active public leadership consumed their attention. Sadness and sickness tested their marriage vows, and they felt oppressed by the burden of things unsaid. Then God breathed awareness and new life upon their marriage, teaching them to make their relationship a priority, helping them "to heighten mutual respect, to accept idiosyncrasies and whims, to be more gentle with each other, and to lift each other up."[106] After they learned these lessons, "The Spirit breathed upon the coals of desire until they flamed red with love."[107] Their marriage was deepened and renewed in a powerful and wonderful way.

We often have an intensive experience of the Refiner's Fire when facing stressful ordeals, circumstances beyond our control, or the loss of what has felt safe and familiar. At such times, our fears, negative beliefs, old wounds, uncomfortable feelings, and painful memories surface from the unconscious, where we have buried them. We see that some of our habits and behaviors have been unwholesome or harmful. Looking at what is revealed and feeling the emotions that arise, if done in the light of God's Love, can release the hold of the past and help us to become more whole.

For early Friends, the Refiner's Fire was a defining aspect of the Quaker experience. Most people in seventeenth-century England believed that human beings live in a fallen, sinful state, cut off from God, influenced by invisible evil forces. Today, the awareness brought by the Refiner's Fire still causes many Friends to see themselves acutely as sinners in need of God's forgiveness and salvation. Visionary experiences and the healing prayers of others helped Kenyan Friend Priscilla Makhino to know Christ experientially. She healed from troubling doubts and a long, mysterious illness. Then she was led into the painful revelations of the Refiner's Fire:

> *I committed my life to my Lord Jesus Christ who led me into the wilderness to be tested by the evil one. I saw clearly that I'm a sinner and I need Jesus to forgive all my sins. I started reading my Bible.*[108]

While some Friends today speak of sin, darkness, and Satan, others speak of the Shadow and the need for psychological awareness and healing past wounds, both personal and social. Belief in human sinfulness and a vision of the world being under the influence of evil forces is not the pervasive worldview it once was. Many contemporary Friends prefer psychological explanations for what is morally wrong in humanity. The power of God that is released within those who seek to be guided by the Light of Christ reveals everything within and without that impedes the movement of the Spirit. Over time, all barriers, whether moral, intellectual, psychological, physiological, social, or cosmic are purged or healed by the Light. Something within humanity resists the process, and for many it takes a major crisis in life to surrender to the spiritual focus and inner work that the Light requires.

Losing one's familiar moorings in life, such as home and family, can be an opportunity for a cleansing and healing experience of the Refiner's Fire. After her second divorce, which coincided with the deaths of some relatives, Linda

Caldwell Lee felt compelled to face unresolved issues. Lee cried while reading a book on father-daughter relationships and felt drawn to spend time in the dark, reviewing her life. She felt anger toward her ex-husband, who had been unfaithful. She dreamed of toppled trees, shattered stones, and the walls of houses falling. Painful things about her life were revealed:

> *I'd failed my sons. I had allowed myself to be pressured to sell my house. . . . I had treated several men badly. I'd chosen men who never saw me as my real self. I had not been good at seeing them clearly either. I had thought I needed to give up myself in order to be loved. Crying felt good and sitting in the dark was strangely comforting.*[109]

Lee started attending a Quaker meeting, meditating, and practicing forgiveness. A process began that led to an opening of her heart:

> *Several nights in a row I dreamed about forgiving others and others forgiving me. It was maybe the fifth day that I wandered in the garden at the Indianapolis Museum of Art and sat on a stone bench to rest. I gazed at the roses. There was a sharp sound and a sudden pain in my heart. "My heart has cracked open," I thought. Tears wet my cheeks. I was amazed and frightened. I looked toward the top of a pine tree feeling that something profound had just happened. A voice that did not seem to be mine said, "Jesus could be your guide." I was amazed. I sat with the feeling of the voice for a while.*[110]

Lee sought spiritual counsel. Later, she asked her ex-husband to meet her outside the art museum, and there she apologized for having added to his pain. It was freeing to say good-bye to him "with kindness."

The Refiner's Fire is often associated with difficult ordeals. For Linda Caldwell Lee, this time of personal reckoning was followed by stressful changes at work and exposure to toxic chemicals. Her immune system became so compromised that she had to wear a mask with an air filter. Unable to continue working, confined to a single room, she began to meditate for long stretches of time, trying a variety of practices. Seeking health and healing took her deep into herself and eventually led to a profound new relationship with God.

When we are led by the Light or forced by painful situations to look at the ways we have harmed others, the Light also prompts us to look at and heal underlying wounds and errors. For many years after his initial experience of divine Presence, Ben Pink Dandelion experienced God affirming his decisions. Eventually, however, God began to nudge him toward greater faithfulness and called him to account for certain actions. When Dandelion made some serious mistakes that hurt people around him, he was forced to look deeply into the reasons for his behavior and to see clearly the injuries he had caused:

> *It is horrible to get it wrong, especially when the consequences are widespread and not easy to mend. The explosion also shone light on other situations in the past where I had been equally lacking.*[111]

Although deeply painful, the experience was both illuminating and freeing:

> *Such revelation is both shocking and liberating, painful and empowering. I have felt deeply sorry, deeply ashamed, and for some time, at the height of being particularly exposed to the anger of others, I lost all confidence. Simple routine tasks were besieged by a sense of having fallen short. The joy and energy disappeared from the everyday. As I try to make amends for my past and live my life now in a new way, I hope I will be forgiven by those I hurt. At the same time, I*

see that I am part of humanity. I have become so much more at ease in the world, less worried about how others may perceive what I do. I have become chatty with strangers, and far more compassionate, more emotional. God loves me, and now Jesus too has a place in my spiritual life, the pure example of a good life, a life well led and well followed, a life of compassion and obedience.[112]

As part of the process of understanding the root causes of his behavior, Dandelion enlisted the help of a therapist who helped him to see more clearly how emotional abuse in childhood shaped patterns of lifestyle and personality that were unhealthy and that prevented him from being true to himself. For some, therapy can be an integral part of the self-revelation and spiritual healing that takes place in the Refiner's Fire; it can help us see more clearly our inner bondage and teach us to open more fully to love and truth. Out of Dandelion's experience came an important insight about his relationship with God, an insight that may be true for most of us today:

I reflect now that I had been taking my relationship with God, and the consequences for my life too lightly, too proudly, keeping God out of the shadow parts of my life by denying their existence, often even to myself. I lost confidence because I was keeping God out of the whole of my life. I feel called now to transparency and integrity in a way I had known in my head before but not realized in my heart. It has taken this kind of shock to make me see: certainly I hope never to need to relearn these lessons.[113]

When we try to ignore the subtle inner promptings to look at how we are not following the truth in our hearts, the promptings become more painful. In his thirties, Parker Palmer suddenly found himself waking up in the middle of the night and staring at the ceiling for hours. He had earned a PhD with the intention of becoming a successful and well-known leader. After five years he burned out from working as a community organizer, activist, professor, and intellectual. He took a year's sabbatical, then accepted a new job as dean of Pendle Hill, a Quaker retreat and study center. This was a better fit for who he truly was, but it did not meet his ideas of high achievement. He plunged into a period of darkness, a depression so painful he sometimes no longer wanted to live.

Many Friends gave Palmer advice or offered words meant to encourage him to look on the bright side. They tried to change or fix him. Others said they knew just how he felt, which to him was clearly not true. All of this only deepened his sense of isolation. A Quaker companion named Bill, however, visited every evening and massaged Palmer's bare feet, usually in silence. Bill was humbly, compassionately present to Palmer as he was. He did not make suggestions but only offered a few simple comments that showed he could glimpse Parker's actual condition, comments such as "'I can sense your struggle today,' or, 'It feels like you are getting stronger.'"[114] These phrases reassured Palmer that someone could see him as he was, "life-giving knowledge in the midst of an experience that makes one feel annihilated and invisible."[115]

His clinical depression, Palmer later wrote,

> was not the sort of spiritual journey I had hoped some day to take, not an upward climb into rarefied realms of light, not a mountaintop experience of God's presence. In fact, mine was a journey in the opposite direction: to an inner circle of hell and a face-to-face encounter with the monsters who live there.[116]

Afterward, he could see that he had been invited many times to look inward but had eluded the call. Only this deep depression finally forced him to stop pursuing fulfillment through outward achievements and turn his attention toward the voice of his soul. He saw that he had been led by ambition to a career not suited for him, and he had deceived himself about the fears that motivated him.

Palmer eventually identified four reasons why he had become so disconnected from the divine Truth within. First, trained as an intellectual, he had learned to live largely in his head. Second, he had followed a form of Christian faith based more on *ideas* about God than on *experience* of God. Third, an inflated ego had masked his fear that he was less than he should be. Finally, he had lived by images of who he *should* be rather than by insight into who he truly was.[117] Palmer began to get well after he looked carefully at the truth about himself and acted on that knowledge. He later saw his descent into the underground as a journey toward God. It was

> *a place where we come to understand that the self is not set apart or special or superior but is a mix of good and evil, darkness and light; a place where we can finally embrace the humanity we share with others. That is the best image I can offer not only of the underground but also of the field of forces surrounding the experience of God. . . . The path to humility, for some of us at least, goes through humiliation, where we are brought low, rendered powerless, stripped of pretenses and defenses, and left feeling fraudulent, empty, and useless—a humiliation that allows us to regrow our lives from the ground up.*[118]

When we open to the Light within, seeing hidden truths about ourselves and the nature of our society can initially be disorienting. People sometimes feel as though they or the world have been turned upside-down or inside-out. Opening to greater spiritual energy and insight can bring so much awareness of what has been hidden or unresolved that some people require help from a therapist. In her book *Dancing with God Through the Storm*, Quaker psychologist Jennifer Elam gives case examples of how an influx of spiritual energy and insight often clashes with the life one has been leading. The need for radical change can cause intense confusion and distressing emotions. For some people, a time of therapy provides needed support to see and feel more deeply, release old wounds, and start reassessing one's true goals and direction in life. Especially for those who have been abused or traumatized in the past, the confrontation with what has been buried or denied can require skilled assistance.

Although psychological help is sometimes needed, for the person who is experiencing the Refiner's Fire, it is not sufficient. Sensitivity to the spiritual dimensions of our experience is also required. Spiritual companions such as Palmer's friend Bill are needed. Elam hopes that Quaker meetings can learn to better recognize and support those whose spiritual journey is taking them through a difficult inward process.

When the Light begins to reveal hidden truth to us, it does not stop with personal, private, inward truths. As discussed in the section on openings, the Light shines on outward realities as well, showing all the ills of society and the deceptions, fears, and uncontrolled cravings from which those ills spring. As we see more clearly the ways in which society perpetuates ignorance and oppression, it becomes painful to continue conforming in the ways we have done before. We see everything in a new light. We see what allows love and truth to flourish and what does not. Following God and Christ requires us to change, and the requirement to change can plunge us more deeply into the Refiner's Fire.

When Elise Boulding traveled to India, she met people living in immense poverty and hardship. As a result, the material excesses and cushy comfort of U.S. suburban culture were difficult to bear when she returned home.

And so I lived in suburbia again. . . . All around me were well-intentioned, socially conscious people, supporting good causes. At Friends meeting on Sunday mornings I would sit in the silence with all these good people, listen to words of kindly mutual encouragement and often poetic insight, and return as they did to the domestic comforts which sealed us all off from the living God.[119]

She experienced what she referred to as "a call to strip." For months she was plunged into a state that nobody around her could understand except to recognize that it was a spiritual crisis. It forced her to reexamine who she was and the purpose of her life.

Nearly every Quaker meeting offers opportunities for silence, personal reflection, intimate conversations, and discussions that encourage the inner work of the Spirit. Giving time for this both in solitude and in community helps the truth in one's heart to be revealed and the work of the Refiner's Fire to take place as painlessly as possible. Quaker retreat and study centers, such as Pendle Hill in Pennsylvania, Woodbrooke Quaker Study Centre in England, Silver Wattle Quaker Centre in Australia, and Ben Lomond Quaker Center in California, are places where Quakers and others can spend a weekend or a longer period of time devoted to allowing the transforming work of God to take place as fully as needed. Parker Palmer writes that the phrase *inner work* ought to be in common use. He stresses the importance of understanding that,

> *inner work is as real as outer work and involves skills one can develop, skills like journaling, reflective reading, spiritual friendship, meditation, and prayer. We can teach our children something that their parents did not always know: if people skimp on their inner work, their outer work will suffer as well.*[120]

Allowing ourselves to see what has been repressed and hidden is something we must do not just for our personal refinement and healing but also for the sake of our community and our world, for what hides in the shadows within ourselves affects others even if we remain ignorant of its existence and effects. Taking time on a regular basis to turn our attention inward and allowing ourselves to ask for and receive help in doing so from family, friends, therapists, spiritual companions, and our faith community are ways that we open ourselves to God's healing and make more room for it in the world around us.

Even though we are called to participate in the process of purification and clarification, it is important to emphasize that the Refiner's Fire is not something under human control. The work of the Light within us and in society is initiated by God. The Light refines things in human consciousness that we will never fully recognize or understand. Much of the transformation that occurs in the divine refining process remains hidden and mysterious. Indeed, we may not always have a sense of God's Presence in it because a lot of it takes place at levels beyond our conscious awareness. The transformation that results when we cooperate and participate is always God's handiwork. Sandra Cronk describes the nature of that transformation:

> *Through being stripped of the usual inward ideas and illusions about ourselves, our world, and even about God, we are able to let go of narrow or false understandings of the nature of human existence which were manufactured out of our fears, hurts, angers, and desires, or were passed along by the social order in which we live. As a result we are able to see more clearly. We are released from enslavement to false expectations and wrong desires. Our lives are now centered in that empty place with God. Out of that new centering comes a freedom to make new decisions, to see new truth, and to enter into a new pattern of life.[121]*

Reflection Questions

The Refiner's Fire

Have inner questions or uncomfortable feelings guided you to look at your life, beliefs, behaviors, and motivations in new ways?

When, if ever, have you felt God, Christ, or the Light showing you things you are doing that are not God's will or not in keeping with love and truth? What is that like?

How have you been freed from unwholesome or sinful beliefs, behaviors, and habits?

Have you been shown how certain ways you participate in society are contrary to the ways of God?

Have new ways of seeing your life or yourself brought about any change within you or in the way you live?

How do you experience becoming less conformed to the ways of the world and less easily controlled by the baser human instincts, such as fight or flight?

Community in the Seventeenth Century

Most early Friends opened to the divine Presence within while in the company of others. In such cases, the surrender to God by a whole group was a great aid to each person. Together they experienced the Light and the direct teaching of the Spirit of Christ. At the same time, they were knit together as a people of God. Those who were alone were drawn to join with a gathered group, or, if no group was nearby, they visited and corresponded with other Children of the Light.

The first Quakers left many descriptions of their collective experiences of God's Presence, which they often described by saying that "the Power of the Lord was over all." One of the most beautiful descriptions was written by Francis Howgill in 1663:

> *The Lord of Heaven and earth we found to be near at hand, and, as we waited upon him in pure silence, our minds out of all things, his heavenly presence appeared in our assemblies, when there was no language, tongue, nor speech from any creature. The Kingdom of Heaven did gather us and catch us all, as in a net, and his heavenly power at one time drew many hundreds to land. We came to know a place to stand in and what to wait in; and the Lord appeared daily to us, to our astonishment, amazement and great admiration, insomuch that we often said one unto another with great joy of heart: 'What, is the Kingdom of God come to be with men?' . . . And holy resolutions were kindled in our hearts as a fire which the Life kindled in us to serve the Lord while we had a being. . . . And from that day forward, our hearts were knit unto the Lord and one unto another in true and fervent love, in the covenant of Life with God. . . . And thus the Lord, in short, did form us to be a people for his praise in our generation.*[122]

A few weeks after his convincement, early Quaker leader Richard Hubberthorne used the metaphor of family to describe the intimate relationship he now felt with others in the Quaker community:

> And to you all the dear family of love, my love is run into you all. You are my relation, father, mother, sisters and brothers, which I must now own and dwell with in amity and love eternally.[123]

Their collective surrender to the will of God was key to the community that developed among early Friends. Supporting one another to persevere in spite of persecution helped create a powerful and loving spiritual bond. In his journal, John Banks wrote that "it was through various trials and deep exercises, with fear and trembling, that on this wise we were made partakers."[124]

These early Quakers experienced church not as a building but as a people gathered by the Spirit. God endows the community, through its members, with all the necessary spiritual gifts. A way of fulfilling the functions of church emerged among them that early Friends called Gospel Order. They had no paid clergy, and all the members of the meeting bore a share of responsibility for ministry, as well as for maintenance of the community. The Spirit required each person to give time and resources to meet needs identified by the corporate body, for the sake of furthering God's work both within the beloved community and in the wider world. Dorothy White urged Friends to surrender to God's Love; in doing so they would be enabled to better love one another, and this would reveal to the world how God was at work among them: "And all must feel the overcoming Life of Love to overcome. . . . and this must convince the World that we are of God, because we love the Brethren."[125]

Early Friends valued unity. They were careful to distinguish true unity in God's loving Spirit, however, from outward conformity in behavior or professed belief. As

Isaac Penington wrote, they saw enforced conformity as a form of spiritual violence, and they recognized that inward unity in God is possible even when there are different outward ways or different degrees of understanding God's will:

> The great error of the ages of the apostasy hath been to set up an outward order and uniformity, and to make men's consciences bend thereto, either by arguments of wisdom, or by force; but the property of the true church government is, to leave the conscience to its full liberty in the Lord, to preserve it single and entire for the Lord to exercise, and to seek unity in the light and in the Spirit, walking sweetly and harmoniously together in the midst of different practices. . . . O! how sweet and lovely is it to see brethren dwell together in unity [Psalm 133:1], to see the true image of God raised in persons, and they knowing and loving one another in that image, and bearing with one another through love, and helping one another under their temptations and distressed of spirit, which every one must expect to meet with.[126]

Almost as soon as the Quaker movement was formed, Friends were called to share the good news that the Light of Christ was within, available to all. Many did this in their own communities and towns. Others were called to travel more widely to share the message. Rarely did they travel alone. Sometimes they traveled in groups, especially those who accompanied George Fox. However, most often they were paired with a traveling partner, which helped each of them to remain connected to the support and discernment of the community. In pairs like Christ's disciples—usually two men or two women, and on rare occasions a married couple—they set off to spread the message of Christ's inward Light. Other Quakers provided hospitality for them along their way, welcoming them into their homes and providing necessities for the journey.

When John Bowne was banished from the colony of New Netherlands in 1662 for hosting Quaker meetings in his home, he was put on a ship to Europe to face the East India Company in Amsterdam. Allowed, however, to get off the boat when it touched land in Ireland, he traveled to London to seek help from the British Quaker community to present his case in Amsterdam. All along his way on foot across Ireland and England, Friends took him into their homes for the night, fed him, brought them to their meetings for worship, and advised of the next places he might find hospitality. He visited imprisoned Friends along his way, bringing them cheer and news of Quakers in the colonies.

Friends in London advised Bowne to seek help from British Friend William Caton, who lived in Amsterdam and spoke Dutch. They wrote a letter to Caton directing him to provide for all of Bowne's needs at their expense. When Bowne reached Amsterdam, Caton helped him to prepare the necessary documents and acted as translator during eleven meetings with the East India Company. With the support of the Quaker community, Bowne was eventually able to obtain religious freedom for the colony of New Netherlands, setting a precedent when that colony fell under British rule and was renamed New York.[127]

After becoming a Quaker, Margaret Fell devoted the rest of her life to nurturing the Quaker community with all the skills and resources at her command. She opened her home, Swarthmore Hall, for regular meetings for worship and provided hospitality to traveling Friends. She also maintained an extensive network of communication, exchanging letters and writing epistles and tracts to communicate the Quaker message. She traveled in the ministry to help Friends feel the bonds of loving community in person and used her connections with Parliament and the King of England to plead for the release of Quaker prisoners. She was one of many "nursing mothers" who helped to maintain the newly forming Quaker community.

Many who publicly proclaimed the Quaker message were put in prison. In those days, prisoners had to provide for their own food and other necessities, so the Quaker community took it upon themselves to visit Friends in prison and provide for their needs for food, bedding, and firewood. They also cared for the families of those in prison. Fell raised funds to support traveling ministers and provide for imprisoned Quakers and their families. In an epistle to Friends, she described how God's Everlasting Love requires all parts of the Quaker body to contribute to the care of those among them who are in need:

> So let that Love constrain you to love one another, and be serviceable to one another, and that every one may be made willing to suffer for the Body's sake, and that there may be no Rent in the Body, but that the Members have the same Care one over another; and where one member suffers, all the Members may suffer with it: and here is the Unity of the Spirit and the Bond of Peace.[128]

Margaret Fell nurtured the bonds of community in numerous practical ways. The community was also nurtured by prayer, which many Friends experienced as a tangible power. During the three years that Katharine Evans and Sarah Chevers were imprisoned by the Inquisition, they were isolated like "owls in deserts, and as people forsaken in solitary places."[129] They came near death during that time but felt upheld by the presence of God and by the faithfulness and prayers of their community. To Friends at home they wrote,

> We did see you our dear friends . . . and did behold your order, and steadfastness of your faith and love to all saints, and were refreshed in all the faithful hearted, and felt the issues of love and life which did stream from the hearts of those

that were wholly joined to the fountain, and were made sensible of the benefit of your prayers.[130]

Community in Our Time

Today, a person's first experience of Quaker community often happens during worship. Many people feel they have come home. Some experience a communion with God that makes them aware of being connected to the others present. During what Friends call a "gathered" meeting, there is a feeling of spiritual power and a sense of Presence. Many present may simultaneously become aware of having been gathered spiritually, as if into one body. The sense of separateness diminishes or even vanishes and Friends feel united, *in God*, with everyone else around them. Minds are hushed and hearts expand. Some sense an increase of tender love for all. Some feel as though the group is lifted into a heavenly plane shimmering with light; others feel as though the group is brought to a great depth, a place of primordial truth and perfect silence. Sometimes a gathered meeting even feels "covered" by the divine Presence, as if a covering has been placed over the group, or as if the air in the room has weight. Such awe-inspiring moments are fortifying.

Evelyn Jadin first experienced gathered worship when she attended a rural Conservative meeting in North Carolina. Worship was already taking place when she and two college friends entered the small, old meetinghouse:

> *The Presence in the silence was already palpable and deep—our entrance did not disturb it. When we sat, we were enfolded by the silence and brought into deep communion with those around us and the Spirit. Throughout the worship I felt the presence of others around me and a greater presence standing over and around us all, bringing us together under it. Through this worship I felt the Presence of the Living Christ.*[131]

85

In Africa, as in many Quaker meetings and churches in the United States, most of the worship is programmed, with songs, Bible readings, sermons given by pastors, and vocal prayers. Hayo Daniella, a third-generation Quaker from Burundi, attends a Quaker church where her father is a pastor. She belongs to a big choir, one of seven in the church. In addition to singing together, each choir practices spiritual disciplines such as fasting and praying. "Being in a choir," Daniella writes, "is about community and commitment."[132] Her church's Sunday morning worship service takes three hours and includes much singing. She often experiences being gathered by the Spirit of Christ during services, especially while singing in the choir:

> *I do personally experience the presence of Christ. Usually when I am singing. And sometimes when I am praying or even occasionally during the preaching. I feel the presence in my body but it's not like any other feeling I ever have. I feel closer to God and close to other members of the choir. We often all feel the feeling at once but in different ways. I forget the rest of the world in that moment. It is just me and the choir and God. It is good that we forget the world at these times. Often members of my choir lead hard lives. Some have been chased out of their house at night by war. But they come to church and sing. Singing heals us. I have recently learned that some Friends call this "being gathered," and that they experience it in the silence. It amazes me that you can have this without the singing.*[133]

When Daniella visited Freedom Friends Church in Oregon, in the United States, she learned that she, too, could experience God speaking to her in silent worship.

In regional Quaker youth gatherings, young Friends find community with each other to be a powerful support for their faith. After a week spent camping, working, and having fun together in the wilderness, Australian Alexa

Taylor experienced a deep bond of community with fellow Quakers. When the young people crowded together on couches in someone's home, their heads resting against each other's shoulders, there was a profound, liberating silence:

It was woven out of friendship so different from what I knew from school back home, where even among friends people would tease and others would storm off, hurt. From our week of testing the waters gently to see if it was safe, there we were, tucked up in a room together, holding each other in silence. People spoke, their voices soft, as though something held tight had been let down and the part behind it was not so loud or so bold, not so easy to let through. . . . I remember it seeming impossibly hard to open that door to bits of myself that had already been so tightly shut. I remember the speeding up of my heart and the trembling of my fingertips as I decided it might be worth a try, to pry it open even a little. And I remember my quiet sense of surprise that the world didn't end when I did.[134]

Opportunities for young Friends to gather with others in their age group are wonderful. It is also important to give them positions of responsibility and leadership in the community as a whole. The joining together of *all* generations in a Quaker meeting is powerful. As a boy, David Mercadante found it unremarkable to attend meeting for worship week after week with the same people, so many from older generations. Looking back, however, he sees how this spiritual community shaped his understanding of God:

The God I believe in is consistent in Grace and Truth, unwavering in Mercy, and dependable in Providence. God is not a shifting force that changes each week with the tides. Rather, my God mirrors the meeting I call home: steady,

dependable, peaceful, and reliable. I appropriate
God as One who brings good order to the chaos,
just as my home meeting brought peace and
stability to my life during many chaotic times.[135]

Divine communion helps to knit meeting members into
a spiritual family. Jessica Easter grew up in a beloved
church community. When it dissolved, she searched for
another. At a Friends meeting, she experienced both the
divine Presence and a beloved community:

In Quakers I have found a community who is
willing to support, nurture, laugh, cry, and
wrestle with me. I have also found a community
to which I can give so much of myself. Don't get
me wrong; it is anything but perfect. We still
struggle with complacency, racism, sexism,
classism, and many other illnesses with which
the wider population must also wrestle.
Nevertheless, I keep catching glimpses of a
sleeping giant among Friends.[136]

God and Christ gather the community, but the members
help one another to live with faith, in God's grace. Friends do
this through listening to each other's stories and affirming
gifts and calls. Gladys Kang'ahi, who has served in many
leadership roles among Quakers in Kenya, describes the
community's crucial role in affirming each person and
sustaining faith:

We need to look, we need to listen, we need to
speak, and we need to touch. We encounter each
other as a people of faith with faith in ourselves
and faith in each other. Each one of us has a
wealth of experiences to share. We need therefore
to affirm each other's gifts, to affirm each other
as full human beings created in the image of God.
We need to listen to each other's struggles. We
have been growing and need to look forward to
growing further in our understanding of

ourselves as a people who have a task, to make this a better world as we continue to minister.[137]

Most religious communities provide accompaniment to celebrate, support, and grieve with each other through life's important transitions: birth, graduation, marriage, death. The Religious Society of Friends offers some special communal ways to share such moments. One of these is the Quaker way of marriage, a sacrament that is witnessed and supported by the community. Quakers believe that it is God that makes a marriage, not a pastor or priest. During a special meeting for worship, the couple rises and speaks their vows to each other in the presence of God and the community. Afterward, in an open period of worship, anyone is able to rise, as moved by the Spirit, and speak aloud a message, blessing, or prayer.

Before a wedding, Quaker meetings provide a clearness committee to meet with the couple and help them determine if, indeed, God is uniting them in marriage. Elizabeth Baltaro and her fiancée Ben met with a clearness committee composed of several meeting members a few months after Ben had proposed to Elizabeth. After a period of silent worship, committee members asked the couple questions about struggles in their current and prior relationships, as well as about their plans for creating a family together. After everyone felt clear that Elizabeth and Ben were, indeed, called to marry, the meeting appointed a different group to help them plan and carry out their wedding. The event was a joyous celebration. The couple felt their marriage was divinely blessed. Baltaro writes:

We were not sure that the actual moment of our marriage would feel like God marrying us. . . . However, when the wedding day came, the experience of the meeting for worship was incredible. Ben and I entered the room with our family members around us, and a large group of friends and family circled around us. I remember the feeling of warmth and calmness, like we were

89

floating in the room. Everything went just as we'd expected, but the emotions and movements I felt within me were much stronger than those I felt during a usual meeting for worship. God was really there with me. All the messages we heard seemed to fit together more perfectly than any meeting Ben or I have ever been to. For us, they were exactly the messages we needed to hear— speaking directly to us in a startling way.[138]

Baltaro is grateful for the way the meeting supported the couple:

Ben and I made our marriage our own, respecting our own values and those of our community. Because of this we feel closer than ever to each other, our meeting, our friends, our families, and God.[139]

Quaker memorial meetings are also special, grace-filled experiences, a way to celebrate the life of a member who has died, to grieve communally, and to be gathered together in God's Love at a time of loss. Like a wedding, a memorial meeting is basically a meeting for worship. Sometimes particular songs or readings are planned in advance. Then, out of the silence of worship, anyone may rise, as led by the Spirit, to share a memory of the one who has died or offer a prayer or speak other words of vocal ministry. In a Quaker memorial meeting, many different facets of the person are shared. The beauty, struggles, love, and wholeness of the person's life are revealed in a poignant way. Those who attend are given a multifaceted view of how God's grace has worked through that individual. All are blessed by the revelation; many leave strengthened with the knowledge that God's grace must be at work in their lives, too, though it takes a community to glimpse the wholeness of that.

Through Quaker community, God draws people closer to a holy and faithful way of life. Individuals give to the community through participation and acts of service. In turn, they receive the supportive environment needed to become who they truly are. A healthy individuality is actually the gift of a healthy community. Thomas Gates writes,

> *True community and true individuality reinforce one another. We believe that the most vital communities are those which do not fear to encourage their members' individuality. At the same time, we believe that authentic individuality is most likely to arise not in opposition to community, but within the matrix of a supportive and nurturing community.*[140]

Rhonda Pfaltzgraff-Carlson discovered that over time she grew into her community like a branch on a vine. Jesus' words in John 15:5 speaks to her of community and her relationship with God through the meeting: *"I am the vine, you are the branches. Those who abide in me and I in them bear much fruit, because apart from me you can do nothing."* She has been surprised to discover how she herself has benefited while serving her meeting and how, in doing so, she has become a part of the meeting in a new way.[141] Through participating in her meeting's jail ministry, she has also found a new dimension of her calling:

> *I have discerned that I am being led to grow more fully into who God wants me to be through one of the meeting's ministries. I know it shouldn't surprise me, but I have a strong tendency to try to 'go it alone,' discrediting my role in the community and not believing that the meeting is God's and that Christ works through the meeting. I thought that I needed to figure out what my spiritual gifts were so I could determine what I needed to do, quite independent of the meeting. Now, I believe that my participation in the meeting has allowed Christ to live in and move through me, so that I, in conjunction with the meeting, might do Christ's work in the world.*[142]

One of the most powerful ways that Friends today experience being gathered into spiritual community is when a group carries out a leading together. *Quaker Theology* editor Chuck Fager felt himself to be part of a people on a spring day in 1967 as he crossed the Canadian border at Fort Erie. He was part of the Peace Bridge, a group of New York Quakers carrying medical supplies into Canada to be shipped to civilian victims on all sides of the Vietnam War. In obedience to a leading, they were defying the law and committing civil disobedience. They announced their intention to the border patrol officers. Fager wrote,

> *I smiled all the way across the bridge, and I remembered especially the warm greetings of the Canadian Friends who met us. That was a very special moment in my young Quaker journey. And in reflecting on what made it so special, this word peoplehood came back into my mind. That walk over the bridge, and the reception we got from Canadian Friends, was the act of a self-conscious people, a group with an identity and a mission; and that day, these realities were clearly in focus for me, if not yet articulated.*[143]

In community, Friends affirm and listen to each other, celebrate and grieve together, and make a joint witness to the world. At the same time, Quakers also annoy and offend each other. Working with each other, making decisions together, and seeking to understand our role in the world brings us into contact with each other's differences and sharp edges. Participating in community often plunges people into the Refiner's Fire. After offending one another, then we are prompted by the Light to improve our ability to communicate. We are provided the opportunity to develop understanding, practice forgiveness and peacemaking, and discover how to serve each other and be served. In the extended family of Quaker community, we can grow in service and become more aware of God as the active principle within ourselves and the others in our community.

For some Friends, the first powerful taste of Quaker spiritual community comes during a meeting for worship for the conduct of business, often simply called a business meeting. This is a corporate practice to discern how God is leading the community to action. In these meetings, Friends practice speaking what they know. Then, letting go of the need to control the outcome, they listen together for God's will. It is one of the most powerful spiritual practices in Quakerism, an essential way in which the Spirit draws a community together into deeper faithfulness. Eden Grace, Global Ministries Director at Friends United Meeting (FUM), says, "A business meeting is an opportunity for sacramental encounter with God."[144]

It's a misperception that Quakers seek consensus. Actually, Friends wait for more than mere agreement about a decision. Together they seek "the sense of the meeting," a collective discernment about the will of God for the group.

Quaker business practice rests on the conviction that, indeed, God does have a will for us and that collectively, through worship, prayer, and attentive listening, we can come to know what that will is. According to Bill Taber, a Spirit-filled meeting for business is, "a hands-on laboratory-like experience in which the whole fellowship comes face to face with the Spirit's demands for the sacrifice of time, treasure, convenience, and prejudice."[145] It is a key practice in the life of a community, he writes, "through which we learn to walk hand in hand with each other and the Spirit out into the world to do the work of committed and obedient disciples."[146]

Sometimes Friends labor with each other for a period of time over decisions that seem insignificant. Even when the meeting community considers a mundane choice such as the kind of carpet to buy, many issues can arise: aesthetic, practical, environmental, economic, and social. There may be something more important going on than the particular decision that needs to be made. Grace says,

God cares about us as a community walking through that process together and the spiritual

93

fruits that can come from seeking deep unity. . . .
So, yes, we say that each and every decision
facing the meeting is a holy and sacred and
sacramental opportunity, that there is no secular
work.[147]

This is a practice that offers a model for the world.

The deep learning that can come from participation in the meeting community is often greatly intensified for those who live together. Elizabeth Ann Blackshine was part of a community she found to be wonderfully transforming during a year spent at Pendle Hill retreat center:

Never had I been so ripe for healing and
transformation than that year and never had I
been so deeply met and supported than at that
time. I attribute it to the many elders who were
there that year. They and other seasoned Friends
offered such a deep holding space, that
unquantifiable quality of cultivating the air of love
in every corner of a space, of having the love
generator on 24/7 that allowed me to heal and
transform deeply, feeling so spiritually and
soulfully held. The willingness to be deeply
vulnerable, exposed, fully present from all Friends
is a big factor. That year at Pendle Hill was such a
beautiful balance of holding on to a core of Quaker
principles, with an encouragement to have
meetings for worship with a concern for just about
any topic one was drawn to. There was such a
wide container for Spirit to fill.[148]

This highly positive experience in Pendle Hill was not matched, however, by Blackshine's experience in a Quaker meeting she attended afterward, which she found "full of the unresolved conflict and prejudices that affect Friends today." As an African American, Blackshine has found similar dynamics in other Quaker groups:

My perception is that it's race-based on both sides.
This is not an accusation but more a shining of

light on a deep wound that all Friends could benefit from looking at and pouring attention to for Spirit to continue to slowly heal. . . . I long for more worship sharing around topics of race and other social barriers that still need enormous healing in the nation and therefore, naturally, still in the Society of Friends.[149]

Many Quaker Meetings and organizations are actively working toward this healing.*

Evan Welkin felt called to visit some of the meetings on the East Coast after his sophomore year at Guilford College. Raised in an independent monthly meeting in Washington State, he wanted to find out how Quaker community worked and what leadership looked like in older, more established meetings. He also hoped to engage Friends in dialogue that would foster vitality and greater unity among those he visited. He bought a motorcycle and traveled over 4,200 miles with a letter of introduction, visiting twenty-nine meetings between Florida and New York City. Staying in the homes of Friends along the way, he had deep conversations with many "incredibly interesting, thought-provoking, eccentric, kind, and inspired people."[150]

In some meetings, he clearly sensed that the members truly cared for one another. He saw they had "clear ways of holding individuals accountable to the group as a whole and did so."[151] The vitality of such meetings reached out into the wider body of Quakerism and the world beyond. Welkin was disappointed, however, not to find this sense of

---

* Blackshine writes that she is "so thankful for the Friends who are doing that on their racial and social justice committees and for Friends like Donna McDaniel and Vanessa Julye whose book *Fit for Freedom, Not for Friendship* has been an enormous resource along this slow journey." Liz Blackshine, April 19, 2013 (12:42 p.m.), comment on Marcelle Martin, "Being Gathered into Community," *A Whole Heart* (blog), April 2, 2013, http://awholeheart.com/ 2013/04/02/being-gathered-into-community/.

vital community or unity in all meetings. It seemed to him that many people are Quakers for "self-centered reasons." Many communities depend upon the heavy involvement of a few Friends who "seemed to bear a disproportionate amount of responsibility for the affairs of their meetings: spiritually, logistically, and energetically."[152] In these meetings, he witnessed the "push and pull of the individual will versus the will of the whole," a struggle or dance "between the individual and the music of the Spirit that animates our lives."[153]

Peggy Senger Morrison urges Friends to go beyond self-centeredness, which is isolating. Transcend loneliness by giving to others, she advises:

> *You may be unlucky in love, but community does not rely on luck. It relies on initiative. You have to get outside of yourself and your feelings and do something to connect. You have to give, and be vulnerable enough to let others give to you. It is hard work, but it works every time.*[154]

Thomas Gates describes four stages of membership. A Quaker meeting, he writes, is first of all a community that provides open-hearted listening, acceptance, and hospitality to newcomers, inviting them to participate fully in the meeting's activities. Second, meeting is a place where people find "a sense of core beliefs, values, and commitments that are understood and shared by all."[155] Telling stories from Quaker history and sharing the experiences of Friends today are ways to help members learn about the common values and beliefs of Friends and how they become manifest in our lives. Third, a Quaker community is a place where members are brought into a deeper relationship with God, both through engagement with one another and through efforts to reshape their lives to fit more fully with a Quaker testimony or to engage more frequently in spiritual disciplines. When Friends experience God guiding them and prompting action, they can seek the support of the community for help with discernment of their next step. Through the members' and attenders' deepening relationship with the Spirit, the meeting becomes a place of transformation. Finally, as Friends learn to surrender to the leadings of the Spirit, the meeting becomes a place of obedience, a community of faithfulness.

The final four elements of the Quaker spiritual journey, Leadings, the Cross, Abiding, and Perfection, are experienced in the stage called Faithfulness.

Reflection Questions

Community

Has spiritual community been essential to your spiritual journey? If so, in what ways?

What claims does God make upon us when we are gathered together into community?

Has your community sometime made claims or placed requirements that are not God-given?

In what ways have you, others, and your meeting been gathered by God into a spiritual unity or community? How has that changed the way you live and love? What, if anything, has stood in the way of that?

How does being part of a gathered spiritual community help us live faithful lives?

Faithfulness

*As many as are led by the Spirit of God, they are
the sons of God.* —Romans 8:14 KJV

During the process of convincement, people see more
clearly the ways that their lives do not conform with God's
loving design, and they learn how to change inwardly and
outwardly to live in accordance with the divine will. Those
who become faithful to the promptings of the Spirit learn
increasingly to serve God's purposes, within their own
homes and communities, and also in the wider world.

Leadings in the Seventeenth Century

Seventeenth-century Quakers spoke of feeling a
"drawing" or receiving an "opening" to do something, or of
having a "weighty exercise" placed upon them. Many wrote
of being "moved of the Lord" or "commanded of the Lord"
to do a particular act. They quoted, *"As many as are led by
the Spirit of God, they are the sons of God."* In court,
William Dewsbury used inclusive language, explaining that
"as many as are led by the Spirit of God, are the Sons and
Daughters of God."[156]

As a person grows in sensitivity to God's Presence,
human behaviors that are contrary to divine Love and
Truth become more evident and more painful to endure.
Those desiring to be faithful may feel a special burden in
relation to some particular need, wrong, or injustice in the
world. This is often described as being "exercised" about
something or as having a "concern" placed upon one. At
the beginning, Quakers felt above all concerned to address
the spiritual alienation and oppression that lie at the root
of all harmful behaviors and unjust social systems.

Those on whom a concern has been placed may
experience God leading them to take some particular
action. Early Friends usually experienced promptings, first

of all, to faithfulness in the particulars of daily life. Barbara Blaugdone, a tutor of children, felt God asking her to give up the fancy clothing and flattering speech that marked a higher social status and then to simplify her diet:

> *As the Evil was made manifest, I departed from it, and willingly took up the Cross, and yielded Obedience unto it, in plainness of Speech and in my Habit [clothing]. . . . And then the Lord caused me to abstain from all Flesh, Wine and Beer whatsoever, and I drank only Water for the space of a whole Year; and in that time the Lord caused me to grow and to prosper in the Truth.*[157]

Ordinary people—farmers, artisans, tradesmen, sons and daughters, mothers and fathers—were led by God to civil disobedience in the form of refusing to pay mandatory tithes to the state church. They also gathered publicly in large meetings for worship, which were forbidden to all groups except the state-sanctioned church. Thousands of Quakers were imprisoned for such things. Other members of the community felt led to offer support to the prisoners and their families.

Concerns, calls, and leadings are not general precepts learned from reading Scripture and listening to sermons. Although early Friends believed that any genuine prompting from God was consonant with Scripture and a holy life, calls and leadings are guided from within by the still, small voice of God or by an inward movement of the Holy Spirit. Seventeenth-century Quakers read stories in Scripture of prophets, saints, and holy people with the understanding that God wanted to work in their lives in the same way. As they surrendered to divine promptings and responded faithfully to the calls and leadings they received, they learned to let God—through Christ—be the initiator of their actions and also the power that made everything happen. In this way, they gradually allowed God to incarnate more fully in the world.

William Caton, raised in the household of Margaret and Thomas Fell, became a Quaker traveling minister at a young age. Soon he was led to bring the Quaker message to Holland. From there, he wrote a letter describing a leading he felt to marry a young Dutch woman named Annekin Diericx:

[I felt a] mighty clear opening of my proffering of my self to take [Annekin's] part in marriage. . . . This thing settled in me, and grew clearer and clearer, neither could I expel it as heretofore I could have done [a] flashing thought which have come as lightenings in some cases, . . . for the longer it continued the more assurance I came to have in my self, of the thing being of the Lord. . . . And in the mean time it came to be shown unto me, how I should proceed in the thing: As first of all . . . I was to propound it to some dear friends to hear and receive their advice . . . and so much subjection I found then in my spirit that if they . . . had no unity with the thing that then I could (I believe) have let the thing have fallen and have rested satisfied in myself about it.[158]

This is among the earliest written descriptions of a Quaker seeking "clearness" about a leading to marriage.

Many early Quakers felt called to leave home and travel in the ministry, speaking, writing, and teaching about a more true and loving way for human beings to live. Elizabeth Hooton, the second Quaker traveling minister, responded boldly to the leading she received and quickly landed in prison. William Dewsbury heard the call years before it was time to leave his family and home. Francis Howgill received his call after surrendering to God's judgment and experiencing a new birth. James Nayler and Marmaduke Stevenson heard God speak to them directly while they were plowing their fields, calling them to leave their homes and travel in God's service. Stevenson's beautiful account of receiving a call to travel to Barbados, which includes many images and phrases from the Bible, echoes the stories of biblical prophets:

As I walked after the plough, I was filled with the love and living presence of the Living God, which did ravish my heart when I felt it; for it did increase and abound in me like a living stream, so did the love and life of God run through me like precious ointment, giving a pleasant smell; which made me to stand still; and as I stood a little still with my heart and mind stayed on the Lord, the Word of the Lord came to me in a still small voice, which I did hear perfectly, saying to me in the secret of my heart and conscience: "I have ordained thee a prophet to the nations." And at the hearing of the Word of the Lord, I was put to a stand, being that I was but a child for such a weighty matter. So at the time appointed, Barbados was set before me, unto which I was required of the Lord to go, and leave my dear and loving wife and tender children. For the Lord said to me immediately by his Spirit that he would be as a husband to my wife and as a father to my children, and they should not want in my absence, for he would provide for them when I was gone. And I believed that the Lord would perform what he had spoken, because I was made willing to give up myself to his work and service, to leave all and follow him, whose presence is with me.[159]

Mary Fisher, an illiterate maidservant, received a call to spread the Quaker message after hearing George Fox speak. She was put in a castle dungeon for reproving a priest. There, fellow Quakers taught her to read and write. After her release, Fisher felt led to take the message of the inward Light of Christ to places where it had not yet been proclaimed: first the seminaries of Oxford, England, and then Puritan Massachusetts. In Oxford the mayor ordered her whipped on the public square. On the island of Barbados, where she stopped on her way to the colonies, she was instrumental in starting a Quaker community. However, when she arrived in Boston with a trunk full of Quaker pamphlets, the Puritan magistrates ordered that she be stripped, searched for signs of witchcraft, and then imprisoned. After Fisher returned home to England, she traveled to Holland.

In 1658 Fisher was one of six Friends, three women and three men, who felt God leading them to travel to Turkey to speak to the sultan. At that time, most in England considered the sultan to be the enemy of Christendom and an incarnation of evil. The British consul in Turkey, skeptical that a visit from Quakers would improve relations between the two countries, tricked the Friends when they arrived in Smyrna, sending them on a boat headed back to Italy. A huge storm arose, and Fisher and two companions persuaded the captain to let them off on a Greek island. These three traveled back to Turkey. Fisher was the only one to reach the sultan's encampment, which was in Edirne (Adrianople). She walked long distances, depending upon the hospitality of the people who lived along the way. Once arrived at the sultan's military encampment, she managed to persuade an official that she had a message from God. She was received in the sultan's sumptuous tent as an "Ambassador of God," and her message was graciously received. Her ministry was the most far-reaching, geographically, of any of the early Friends.

Fisher, Hooton, Fox, Dewsbury, Howgill, Nayler, and Stephenson were all imprisoned multiple times for following their calls and leadings. Each time these courageous Friends were released from prison, they listened for the next leading. Sometimes they struggled, but then they obeyed.

Leadings in Our Time

Contemporary Friends often speak of receiving leadings. Many have sensed God leading us to take particular actions and have obeyed as faithfully as possible. In this we share a common understanding with the first Quakers. Recognizing and following God's leadings is fundamental to the Quaker way and is part of how God helps Friends grow in the spiritual life. As Thomas Gates writes,

> A major tenet of Quaker spirituality is the belief that leadings are the single most important way that God is potentially present in our lives. . . . Whatever the outward results of our leadings, they always demand from us spiritual growth, and even transformation. . . . Only when we are willing to put ourselves in situations beyond our own power to control can the transforming power of God become fully manifest in our lives.[160]

Leadings can be part of the work we do day by day and are often expressed in our relationships with the people we know. They can take the form of single actions prompted by the Spirit or be part of a larger call on our lives. When Friends commit to a life of faithfulness, they may be led into a new profession or line of work in which ministering to others has a wider scope. Or, they may find ways in their current occupations to bring more and more of God's Love and Truth to others. At the beginning of Quakerism, the term *ministry* was applied primarily to those who preached, prophesied, taught, or encouraged the life of faith. Today, Friends understand that any occupation can become ministry if it is undertaken in response to a call or leading from God and is an effort, in whatever way, to make God's Love manifest or to bring about a world more in keeping with God's ways.

As in previous centuries, many Quakers in our time receive leadings to travel among Friends to help one another grow in the life of faith. We may not know what we

103

will be led to say or whom our ministry might touch. The task, now as always, is to listen for the inner Guide and to be faithful. When Bill Samuel was invited to travel to a gathering at a distant Quaker meeting, he felt led to attend but did not know the purpose. During a meeting for worship, he sought further clarity and sensed that a particular person was to be his traveling companion. A tenuous train of events led to an opportunity for timely communication with this person, who felt clear to accompany him. As it turned out, this companion provided great assistance as the experience unfolded. The meeting involved concern for a Friend who was imprisoned for a matter of conscience. Only after attending the gathering and speaking as prompted did Samuel understand the purpose for which he had been led to attend. He wrote,

> *I had a perspective on the matter underlying the called meeting . . . that no one local had and that the Friends gathered much needed. I was able to share with them . . . a sense of God's victory in the situation which they had not had.*[161]

The experience of discerning and following this leading confirmed for Samuel some understandings Quakers have held about the nature of faithfulness to God's promptings:

> *One is that you may not understand why you are called to something, but that does not relieve you of the need to follow the leading. In fact, that produces greater reliance on Divine guidance as you cannot accomplish the purpose through your own will, because you do not know the purpose. Secondly, it confirmed the wisdom that generally someone traveling in the ministry should have a traveling companion as an aid to their faithfulness. I certainly felt the value of this quite strongly in this instance.*[162]

In all the daily details of life, being led by the Spirit can be a moment-by-moment experience. We may be nudged to speak or connect, serve, confront a problem, or address a need. Leadings can relate to how we obtain food and energy, modes of transportation we use, our clothing and appearance, and where we live. Sometimes people are led to make changes that are not outwardly evident. At other times, visible changes show something about the inward, spiritual change that has taken place. Some contemporary Friends have experienced a leading to wear plain clothing, but there is no standard way of doing so among Quakers today. Each person must listen to discover how they are led. Among a small subset of Conservative Friends, the men wear hats and dark pants while the women wear dresses and caps. For most Quakers today, plain dressing means simple, inexpensive clothing, often from second-hand stores. For some, it means not wearing jewelry or makeup.

When Jessica Easter began to receive internal messages to wear clothes that expressed her faith, she was not sure how to do this. She dreamed of wearing a head covering like those worn by observant Jews during prayer and started wearing a kippah. She sensed, however, that this was not what was required. Next, she decided to dress simply, in clothing from a thrift shop. However, the clothes she bought fell apart very quickly. In seminary, she became friends with a Quaker who wore plain dress. He told her where he got his plain clothing, and she ordered some for herself. For most occasions she now wears a white shirt with plain collar, black or gray pants, and a vest. She even wore this plain clothing to her graduation ceremony, where her classmates and professors were dressed in traditional caps, gowns, and academic regalia.

"I believe wearing plain clothes derives from a spiritual leading to mirror the inward transformation that has taken place," she explains. "Also, it prevents me from putting on masks. I'm the same Jessica at a fancy dinner as I am working with the homeless on the streets of Chicago."[163] In warm weather, she wears t-shirts, some of them colorful.

Some leadings involve taking a one-time action. Following a leading, however, may be a step toward new commitments. God prompts Friends to notice a need and to respond in a particular way, often with a small act. Doing so creates greater awareness, followed by a leading to take another step, and then another. For nine years, Eileen Bagus tutored inmates in the women's cell block of a local incarceration facility for people who had committed drug-related felonies. She taught math to help them pass the GED exam, an alternative to a high school diploma. Occasionally, she also provided emotional support to someone going through a crisis. After nine years, she began mentoring a former student who wanted to go to college after release from prison. When Bagus read a biography of nineteenth-century Quaker Elizabeth Fry's prison ministry, she noted that it started with a small act of kindness and grew until it led to widespread change in the British prison system. Bagus felt led to support this prison inmate and her dreams for a better life:

> *For myself I have never been comfortable with intense activism and demonstrations to achieve systemic change in society; it scares me. But I can easily relate to kindness to an individual. It took me months to slowly win her trust, until she introduced me to her children's father and allowed me to visit their apartment. Her little girl was napping on the living room floor. I realized they had almost no furniture and kept their clothes in plastic bags and wash baskets. Over time I rounded up some furniture from Quaker friends, then clothes and toys. It began to dawn on me that Elizabeth Fry started to make changes in people at Newgate Prison who were thought to be unreachable by using personal resources from her own family, relatives, and Meeting. I bought a small foreclosed house in an online auction, rehabbed it with help from my children, some members of my Meeting, and some paid workers. Then I sold it to this family on a short term land contract with payments lower than the rent for their previous apartment.*[164]

106

Three years after her release from prison, despite difficult economic pressures, the woman had completed her second year of payments on the house and stayed in the same job even through two pregnancies. Her partner was also working. Both looked forward to owning the house outright in seven more years. Community Meeting in Cincinnati, Ohio, provided a support committee for Bagus's prison ministry work. Some members of the meeting were encouraging and were themselves inspired to perform similar acts of helpfulness, but others felt that such support should only be done through social agencies.

Following a leading helps one to grow spiritually and sometimes brings unexpected blessings. After Deborah Saunders heard a group of traditional chiefs from Ghana speak powerfully about atonement and reconciliation, she felt God leading her to continue a dialogue with them and to share their message with young people. With support from her meeting and also a larger Quaker body, in 1997 she accompanied a multiracial group of high school and college students to Ghana to help them develop leadership skills and better understand the Quaker testimonies of peace, equality, and community. In the process, the group gained a clearer vision of what a multiracial, multicultural global society could be like.

In 1998, Saunders became executive director of the Fihankra Project, whose mission is to "reconnect African Americans with their ancient cultures and to build racial harmony among young people of different ethnic groups."[165] Because of this work, the National House of Chiefs in Ghana installed Saunders as an elder among them, a "Queenmother of Unity." This recognition is among the highest honors one can receive in Ghana. The responsibilities include giving counsel to the elders and chiefs and instruction to women and their children, precisely the tasks to which Saunders has felt God calling her. The honor she received brought profound spiritual healing for Saunders:

Never in my life have I felt so humbled. It was a time of healing, a time of cleansing. It was as if all my ancestors descended upon me and washed all the degradation and internalized shame from my being. My past was not one of just being the descendant of slaves. I was indeed descended from kings and queens, and I had been brought back to my homeland to reclaim that which I lost.[166]

Following the leadings of the Spirit can precipitate major life changes. John Fitch was attending seminary in Richmond, Indiana, when he received a leading to buy a run-down, low-cost house in a poor neighborhood and begin a ministry to the people who lived in the area, especially to the mentally ill and to adolescent boys who were not finding a place in society. He gave them somewhere to live and training in repairing houses and maintenance work. Over time, he learned how this leading was also a form of peace work, different from the political action he had contemplated after working in Nicaragua:

I got really discouraged trying to talk to people about peace. When I started my ministry on North 11th Street, I decided I would do less talking and more showing. I realized I was probably not going to see world peace in my lifetime, but on this corner I could work to bring the Kingdom of God down and have it be a microcosm as an example of what the rest of the world could do. I've stopped a lot of fights by just running out the door and shouting "Hey, stop that!" People seem so shocked they have stopped fighting and nobody's beaten me up yet. We also provide sanctuary where people being abused can run to. We've had quite a few bloodied people come barreling though the front door asking for help with their abusers in hot pursuit. But, somehow people have a sense of church grounds being off limits to pursue someone in the traditional sense of sanctuary. Sometimes the perpetrators stand on the sidewalk and heckle the victim but so far nobody's dared come in. I think our presence in the neighborhood has calmed things down significantly to where it is less often that we see fighting on our corner.[167]

It can be difficult to know for sure whether a prompting to action comes from God or from another source. We are motivated by a multitude of impulses and beliefs, many of them unconscious and some deeply embedded by our culture and upbringing. Therefore, Quakers generally test their leadings with others. If a leading comes from God and not merely from an internal motivation, others who are attuned to the Spirit can also sense its source. An important question in discerning a leading is to ask if it leads to the fruits of the Spirit named in Galatians 5:22: love, joy, peace, patience, kindness, goodness, faith, gentleness, and self-control. Does the leading fulfill God's purposes rather than the desires of the ego?

From the beginning of Quakerism, those led to ministry beyond their own community have frequently traveled with another Friend for support in both practical and spiritual matters. Sometimes the traveling companion is another person with a gift for vocal ministry. Many times, however, the companion has gifts as an elder. Elders have responsibility for the spiritual care and nurture of a meeting community. They are gifted in discernment and help others to sense the movement of the Spirit in a group or in a leading. In addition, elders pray for those following a call to ministry. They help Friends to discern their calls and then sometimes accompany them as the ministry unfolds, helping them to remain close to the inward Guide while speaking, teaching, preaching, witnessing, participating in civil disobedience, or facilitating a workshop or retreat. They address both spiritual and practical needs and are attentive to the movement of the Spirit in those receiving the ministry, offering counsel or prayer when needed. After an occasion of ministry, they help the minister to reflect on the experience and prayerfully deal with the aftereffects of having given themselves over in service to the Spirit.

Cathy Walling and Elaine Emily are two Friends whose gifts as elders have been recognized by their communities. They often accompany those who travel with a prophetic message or ministry to share. When Emily was invited to travel among Friends in Australia in 2007 to teach about eldering, Walling accompanied her in the role of elder. During one day-long workshop, Walling sat in silent prayer for six hours. Emily's ability to bring forth the teaching needed by that particular group on that day was assisted by the "spiritual grounding" provided by the elder's praying. In a Pendle Hill pamphlet about their travel together in Australia, Walling wrote,

> *Yokemates is a term that has emerged for us in naming the experience of working together in service to the Spirit to liberate the message. We were co-leading the workshop; in this case Elaine was serving in the minister function, and I was in the elder function. It has been our experience, in spiritually accompanying over one hundred Friends between the two of us, that eldering provides fuller, richer, truer liberation of the message for the community's benefit.*[168]

Quakers today often use clearness committees when they need help to discern their leadings. A group of Friends gathers to prayerfully listen to the individual who senses a leading, to help him or her discern if and how God may be calling them to take action. In addition, some meetings also provide support or oversight committees for those called to an ongoing form of ministry or witness. A growing number of Friends take part in mutual spiritual accountability groups that help one another with ongoing discernment as a call or leading develops over time. Asking for support with discernment can be an important step in a

Friend's spiritual journey, part of the process of offering one's life in the service of divine Love and Truth.

Sometimes Friends need and receive financial support to follow their leadings. Kenyan Quaker Priscilla Makhino heard a call to travel in the ministry not only in Africa but also in Britain and the United States. Friends from her home meeting and from around the world provided essential support:

> *The New Foundation Fellowship Friends helped me discover God's calling. They gave me many books that help me understand the early Quaker message of Jesus Christ. They paid for all my trips overseas. They arranged my travels in America and England. They affirmed me as a servant of God. They have been a great encouragement to me. These Friends supported me in every area of life during a time of catastrophe when everything my family tried failed; when our cattle and chickens died, and all the crops in the farm failed. We were very poor yet we had enough for all the family members. Although my monthly, quarterly, and yearly meetings were not able to sustain this ministry financially, they always gave me a travel minute and prayer.*[169]

When Friends become sensitive to injustice in society, they may feel God leading them to make others more aware of that injustice. The leading may be to an action as simple as writing letters and sending petitions to elected officials, writing for publication, or holding a vigil or public demonstration. Since the beginning of Quakerism, however, Friends have sometimes been called to actions that involve civil disobedience.

African American Bayard Rustin was a member of a meeting in New York City when World War II began. Like many other Quaker men, he registered as a conscientious objector. A year later, however, he was troubled by his awareness that conscription itself was not consistent with what Jesus taught. In 1943, he wrote a letter to his draft board explaining why he could not submit to an order from the Selective Service to become a soldier. All his reasons, he wrote, stemmed from "the basic spiritual truth that men are brothers in the sight of God." Therefore, war is wrong. And conscription is a violation of the freedom to "act on the degree of truth that one received, to follow a vocation which is God-inspired and God-directed." Then, he explained that God had given him a leading—a call, a higher vocation—that he must follow:

> *Today I feel that God motivates me to use my whole being to combat by nonviolent means the ever-growing racial tension in the United States; at the same time the State directs that I shall do its will; which of these dictates can I follow—that of God or that of the State? Surely, I must at all times attempt to obey the law of the State. But when the will of God and the will of the State conflict, I am compelled to follow the will of God.*[170]

For following his conscience, Rustin spent three years in segregated federal penitentiaries, where he followed his leading by nonviolently fighting the racism he found there. After his release, he continued working for the end of racial discrimination. Rustin was among many twentieth-century Friends who boldly risked arrest and imprisonment, in order not to cooperate with unjust laws and to draw attention to dangerous or unjust public policies.

In the twenty-first century, Friends are also feeling led to civil disobedience. For twenty years of her adult life, Quaker author and teacher Eileen Flanagan made personal efforts to live in earth-friendly ways. A shift began to happen after she received a phone call from a friend in Africa, where she had served as a Peace Corps volunteer. Her friend made her aware of the devastating impact of climate change on people living in Botswana. With support from her Quaker community, Flanagan followed a leading to travel there. She saw how rising temperatures and water shortages will have a harsher effect on the world's poorest people and realized that her efforts to reduce her personal and family energy consumption are not enough.

"What the world's hungry need," she wrote, "are big changes from big institutions and people bold enough to call for them."[171] She became more sensitive to the great hazards of American culture's current push to extreme extraction practices like mountaintop removal and to the devastating effects on the environment of burning dirtier fuels, such as oil from tar sands, instead of developing clean energy technologies. A deeper level of commitment was born. "I came home feeling that I was being led to show more courage, act more boldly, and more publicly in my leading to work for climate justice."[172]

Flanagan became active with the Earth Quaker Action Team (EQAT), which was protesting PNC Bank's financial support of mountaintop removal in Appalachia. Flanagan also felt nudged by the Spirit to represent EQAT when representatives of organizations across the country participated in a protest at the White House in an effort to persuade President Obama to veto the Keystone XL pipeline. Handcuffing herself to the White House fence and going to jail, along with almost fifty other activists, was a joyful experience for her. What followed were many opportunities to speak with the press about the concern God had placed upon her. As an active participant in EQAT, Flanagan continued to participate in public actions to draw attention to environmental dangers and to pressure PNC Bank to stop financing the destruction of mountains and Appalachian communities.* In March 2015, five years after EQAT's campaign began, PNC bank

---

* For Eileen Flanagan's account of how she became engaged in environmental activism, see her book *Renewable: One Woman's Search for Simplicity, Faithfulness, and Hope* (Berkeley: She Writes Press, 2015).

publicly announced they were going to pull out of financing mountaintop removal.

An individual following God's promptings can be an instrument for great change. When a community supports an individual's leading, more power can flow. It can be even more effective, however, when a community is led to take action together. When that happens, many individual leadings combine in the context of the whole community's faithfulness.

In the 1970s, the City of Philadelphia demolished the building owned by the American Friends Service Committee (AFSC) in order to build a roadway. Three Quaker organizations then pooled resources to build a modern brick office building called Friends Center adjacent to a historic meetinghouse where abolitionists, women's suffrage organizers, and protestors of the Vietnam War had met to organize. This building was just blocks from City Hall. Thirty years later, Friends Center needed major renovations. Quakers were by then aware that the ways most buildings are heated, cooled, and lighted contributes more to climate change than gas-burning automobiles. It seemed morally imperative to make the building more friendly to the environment.

As a community, Quakers invested the effort and money to install solar panels and geothermal wells for heat and cooling, created a system to collect and use storm water, made more natural lighting available to interior spaces, and created a green, growing roof to help cool the building and the city. The building can now be heated and cooled without the use of fossil fuels. It was awarded a platinum LEED rating, the highest possible. Tours are now offered to those who want to learn about green renovations. In Washington, D.C., the Friends Committee on National Legislation renovated their Civil War-era building to meet LEED standards, too, becoming the first green building on Capitol Hill.

These buildings provide a space both for the Quaker community and for Spirit-led action on behalf of the world's needs. In 2011 Friends Center and the adjacent Race Street Meetinghouse in Philadelphia were put at the service of a people's movement. In September 2011, Occupy Wall Street protestors began camping out in New York City's Financial District to protest the shocking income gap between the "one percent" (the most wealthy people) and the rest of the population. Protest groups in more than nine hundred cities across the world joined in. People camped out together in public places and gathered daily to make decisions by consensus. Committed to nonviolence, the movement was supported by people from all walks of life. Many who did not camp out brought food, blankets, tarps, tents, and other supplies for those who did.

In Philadelphia, an Occupy encampment began around City Hall in October. Within days, the AFSC, Friends Center, and Central Philadelphia Monthly Meeting collectively granted the Occupiers use of their centrally located kitchen, bathrooms, conference rooms, computers, and worship room. Soon, 1,500 meals were being prepared in the Friends Center kitchen each day and served in the encampment. Members of several area meetings volunteered to be hospitality coordinators. The protesters who used the building were orderly and respectful of the site. Meetings between Occupy leaders and city officials were held at Friends Center, as well as trainings on nonviolent direct action.

The AFSC, working with other local spiritual leaders, erected an Interfaith Tent beside City Hall. It was a place for sanctuary, spiritual counseling, meetings, trainings, worship, and religious services. Quakers and others took two-hour shifts providing a presence there. Individual Friends and entire Quaker families camped around City Hall for one or more nights. On the first Sunday of the encampment, fifty Friends from seven area Quaker meetings and organizations held an open-air meeting for worship on a concrete concourse next to City Hall. On subsequent Sundays during the encampment, a meeting for worship was held there from 11 am until noon. One

Friend testified to the palpable Presence during those open-air gatherings:

> *Two homeless men became regular participants in the worship, Paul and Ciro. Paul even became a regular contributor to the verbal ministry. . . . People up above us, in the kind of balcony of the street level courtyard, sometimes even passers-by, would participate, delivering messages or just pause and join us for a moment or two. . . . One consistent aspect of the worship, that grew stronger as time moved forward, was the oneness, the wholeness of it. The deepening silence that contained and embraced the noises that in other circumstances may have seemed to interrupt it, and the speaking, the sharing, the praying, the storytelling, the weeping, and the singing, formed a seamless whole.*[173]

The Monthly Meeting of Friends in Philadelphia (whose meetinghouse was on Arch Street) offered Occupiers use of their grounds during the fall. The following July, when the national Occupy reunion came to Philadelphia, they again offered their grounds as a place of refuge. Portable toilets were installed, and for six days meeting members took shifts acting as hosts and maintaining the agreement that the parking lot and grounds were a worship space. Afterward, the clerk of the meeting, Robert Hernblad, wrote about the lessons for the meeting community:

> *The level of involvement quickly expanded to other members after that first meeting on Sunday, and grew in energy and scope as the days passed and more members joined the effort to make decisions in a timely manner. . . . After the Occupiers left for New York City, I went around to our community members to recognize their many contributions. They replied, again and again, that it wasn't about them; "Robert, you don't get it, this was the*

meeting," was the shared refrain. This spiritual energy brought us together to meet an extraordinary event. We may have helped the Occupiers—I think we did—but we also ended up reaching out to each other. We became stronger as a meeting because we nurtured and responded to each others' gifts and talents.[174]

Friends today are also committed to joining with those of other faiths to work for justice, peace, and healthy communities. In 2008, Quakers in the Philadelphia area joined with members of the Church of the Brethren and the Mennonite Church—all of them historic peace churches—to convene "Heeding God's Call: A Gathering on Peace." Three hundred people of faith from fifteen different congregations participated in four days of worship, prayer, talks, and conversations aimed at discovering how they could work together for a more peaceful world. At the end, an interfaith organization was created called Heeding God's Call. Their mission was to reduce gun violence, and they began by asking local gun dealers to sign a code of conduct designed to reduce illegal gun trafficking that had been created by a national coalition of mayors in the hope of reducing gun violence.

In Philadelphia, Colosimo's Gun Shop was known to have sold the greatest number of guns used in local crimes by people who did not obtain the guns legally. After weeks of talks with the owner, who refused to agree to the code of conduct, Heeding God's Call organized weekly prayer vigils in front of the shop, drawing public attention to the problem of gun trafficking. For nine weeks, people of different faiths participated. At one event, twelve were arrested for peacefully blocking the entrance to the shop. The vigils and arrests drew media attention and put increased public pressure on the federal government, which was holding evidence of ten illegally obtained guns used in crimes that had been originally purchased at Colosimo's gun shop. When charged with gun trafficking, the owner pleaded guilty and closed his shop. Editorials in local Philadelphia papers noted the effective link between public witness, "prayer power," and legal action.

Quaker Noah Baker Merrill was one of the twelve people of faith arrested for civil disobedience in front of the gun shop. His testimony in court, along with the testimony of others, persuaded the judge that their peaceful witness was not a crime. They were acquitted. For years, Merrill has traveled widely among Friends bringing a sobering but hopeful message of prophetic renewal, asking Quakers to look at points in our history when we have "outrun our guide" or stopped listening to the Guide altogether in our eagerness to follow our own ideas of what God wants. Merrill's ministry has been supported by his Quaker meeting in Putney, Vermont, and he testifies to the importance of community in discerning each other's leadings and supporting one another in faithfulness. He is one of many Friends calling Quakers to participate in the collective act of giving birth spiritually to what God wants to bring into the world now:

> *Together, we're charged with helping midwife the birth of newness among us, both inwardly and outwardly. Friends in our time are hearing this. We're rediscovering and reclaiming the gift of spiritual midwifery embodied in the motion of "eldering"—of drawing out one another's gifts and helping them to be grounded and offered faithfully—something that is bringing renewed life and depth to our worship and our corporate life as Friends. And we are called to bring this communal participation, this trusting that we can be made so much more together than we are alone, more than the sum of our parts, into our witness and service in the world. This is a time when it seems the whole Creation cries out to midwife its own liberation, to come more fully alive again.[175]*

Reflection Questions

Leadings

What leadings have you experienced about how to live?

When have you felt led by the Spirit to undertake a particular action, big or small?

How have you responded to leadings? Have you resisted a leading?

How did you know you were experiencing a leading from God and not being motivated by something else?

What helps you test a leading and respond faithfully?

If you followed your leading, what were the fruits?

Have you participated in a leading that was for the community?

The Cross in the Seventeenth Century

If any man will come after Me, let him deny himself and take up his cross daily, and follow Me.

—Luke 9:23 KJV

Following the leadings of the Light ultimately brings joy and great blessing, but early Quakers referred to following God's promptings as "living in the cross." The power they found in practicing their faith came from surrendering their own wills to the Love and Truth and Power of God, to the inward Guidance of Christ. Rather than worship crucifixes or other images of what Jesus suffered long ago, they urged people to attend to the way that the living Christ, the Light within, was calling people to take up their own cross every day.

For early Friends, living in the cross involved obeying God's will in all aspects of life. In an epistle advising people how to conduct their labor and trades, George Fox wrote: "Deny yourselves, and *live in the cross* of Christ, the power of God, for that destroys injustice." In the context of their livelihoods, living in the cross meant to "do that which is just and righteous, uprightly and holily; in that you will have peace, and see God."[176] For Quakers in the seventeenth century, at a time when most prices were negotiable and the gullible were often cheated, this meant charging fair, fixed prices to everyone, even if that meant less profit for themselves.

Patiently enduring the Refiner's Fire, on God's timetable instead of one's own, was part of surrendering to God's will and living in the cross for the early Quakers. Isaac Penington noted that people are eager to receive power from God as quickly as possible. Instead, one must first endure the humbling sight of all the ways that one has followed what is contrary to God. This requires patience:

Wait patiently the Lord's leisure. Be not hasty after life and salvation in the will of the flesh; but leave the Lord to choose his own season for the showering down of his mercy and blessing. The Lord will not [quickly] entertain that spirit which hath adulterated from him (prostituting itself to strangers, and defiling itself), into his bosom; but there must be a time of sorrow, a time of purifying and cleansing. The soul must know and feel that it hath been an evil thing and bitter, that it hath forsaken the Lord, the living fountain of living mercies, and hath sought life from vanities, and among dead idols. And all the idols must be thrown away, and the heart washed from that nature that ran after them, and become a pure virgin, to bear and bring forth the living seed; and by faithfulness to that seed, and waiting in that seed, in the Lord's season it shall receive the mercy, and the blessing, and the inheritance which belongs to that seed.[177]

Even after one has surrendered to God in many ways and a great deal of transformation has taken place, even after the Light begins to shine more and more clearly through an individual, deeper levels of purification are needed. For example early Quaker leader James Nayler, a charismatic preacher, skillful writer, and gentle man, was seen by many as a perfect example of a Christ-like person. Nonetheless, he succumbed to temptation during a time of great stress and confusion. When the Puritan leader of England's new commonwealth was considering accepting the kingship, Nayler and a group of Friends reenacted the entrance of Jesus into Jerusalem on a donkey. They believed that God was leading them to do this as a sign of the coming of Christ within all. It is impossible to know for sure whether or not God asked these friends to perform this reenactment. What is evident, however, is that the discernment of Nayler and his companions was clouded, and their enactment was marred by motivations and actions that did not come from God. A public scandal ensued that brought shame to the Quaker movement and increased persecution. Nayler received a humiliating and nearly fatal punishment, followed by imprisonment. He suffered greatly in prison, mostly in solitude, and gradually came to see how he had strayed from the path.[*]

Nayler accepted God's chastisement. God did not abandon him but provided comfort and guidance. In the last two years of his shortened life, he wrote again about the spiritual journey, urging the faithful to rejoice "in the power of Obedience." He urged Friends to exercise "a diligent, watchful, patient meekness, feeling the godly Principle moving, and following it in faith and obedience in all things."[178]

Early Friends contended that most people "fly the cross" and ignore difficult truths revealed by the Light rather than accept painful revelations about themselves. The experience of accepting humbling truth about oneself and enduring the process of purification feels like a kind of death. In modern psychological terms we might say that the false self is dying or the ego is losing its overriding control. Our prior ways of thinking and behaving, the person we have known ourselves to be, and the ways we have exercised control in the world— all of this is being transformed and coming to an end. In surrendering to God's will and guidance, we surrender control of our lives.

Although early Friends maintained that human beings were originally created with a divine nature, they believed that most people lived in the fallen state that they called "the first man." Margaret Fell described such people as

---

[*] The full story of the reenactment of Palm Sunday by James Nayler and a small group of other Friends is complicated. Many scholars have struggled to understand and explain what happened. Some of the best efforts are by Quaker historian Douglas Gwyn in *The Covenant Crucified* and Harvard scholar Leo Damrosch in *The Sorrows of the Quaker Jesus.*

> *the disobedient ones, that will not stoop to the Light of Christ, and his Power & cross in them, but will live in the liberty of the flesh, where they may exercise their fleshly liberty, Pride and Ambition, Superfluity of Naughtiness, vain Glory and Arrogancy, Voluptuousness, Pomp and Vanity of the World.*[179]

Living in the cross means bringing even natural aspects of life under the control of the Spirit. The body is holy, but it can be driven by strong urges. In the seventeenth century all forms of overpowering desires or addictions were called *lusts*. Early Quakers believed that those who did not follow the guidance of the Light were bound by their lusts and temptations. It was only possible to live in just and holy ways by surrendering to Christ's power within oneself. The cross of Christ, Fell wrote, "is the power of God to crucify the affections and the lusts [of] the World, and the flesh, and the Devil."[180]

The Light of Christ reveals that many things not generally considered "wickedness" by worldly standards are in opposition to God's Love and Justice. The first Friends felt clear that wearing fancy clothing with expensive lace and buttons and finery was contrary to God's will. Such attire was a way of showing one's wealth and maintaining class distinctions, contrary to the inherent spiritual equality of all people. Honor was due only to God, not to people of a higher social rank, so all mannerisms intended to honor another person as more worthy than oneself, such as bowing, tipping the hat, and using the plural "you" for a single person, were actions contrary to God's will. Living in the cross required refusing to do such things.

Wearing plain clothing and using direct, honest language brought mockery, scorn, and persecution upon Quakers. Their refusal to offer flattering language and gestures enraged judges, magistrates, and members of the nobility and gentry. Many Friends spent long months in prison for refusing to take off their hat or address a member of the gentry with a title or flattering words. Mary Penington

123

struggled for months after she understood that the Light was asking her to give up the outward signs of her social class. Finally, she and her husband obeyed what they felt God asking them to do and "took up the cross." They started wearing plain clothing, used plain speech, and publicly attended Quaker gatherings. For this they were mocked, scorned, and persecuted, even by family members, who took their property away from them:

> *We became obedient to the heavenly voice, receiving the truth in the love of it, and took up the cross to customs, language, friendships, titles, and honour of this world; and endured, patiently, despisings, reproaches, cruel mockings, and scornings, from relations, acquaintances, and neighbors; those of our own rank, and those below us, nay, even our own servants. To every class we were a by-word; they would wag the head at us, accounting us fools, mad, and bewitched. As such, they stoned, abused, and imprisoned us, at several towns and meetings where we went. This not being enough to prove [test] us . . . it pleased the Lord to try us by the loss of our estate, which was wrongfully withheld from us, by our relations suing us unrighteously. . . . We were put out of our dwelling-house in an injurious, unrighteous manner. Thus we were stripped of my husband's estate and a great part of mine.*[181]

Quakers were imprisoned for refusing to pay tithes to the state church, for publicly speaking about their faith and condemning injustice, and for gathering in public meetings for worship. In following the leadings of the Light, many Friends lost possessions, sometimes even the necessities for earning their livelihood such as looms and farm animals. Thousands were beaten or put in prison, and hundreds died. To follow God, they had to be willing, if called, to do things contrary to the body's desires for comfort, safety, and economic prosperity. The suffering they endured was not punishment for their own faults or sins. It was participation in the cross of Christ, a way of helping to bear the burden of the world's lost and sinful condition, as Christ did. Early Friends who lobbied for fairer treatment of Quakers and for Friends' release from imprisonment put together accounts of their sufferings to show to the king, members of Parliament, and others in government. These accounts fill several volumes.[182]

After release from her first imprisonment in 1651, Elizabeth Hooton was glad to return to the family farm. Having tasted persecution and suffering, she was tempted to stay safely at home. However, when she listened inwardly and hushed the loud voices of her fears, temptations, and earthly desires, she heard the quiet voice of Christ calling her back to the traveling ministry. This voice battled with another one that whispered that she had done enough, suffered enough already. In a letter she later wrote to some Friends, Hooton described the struggle:

> *O dear friends, when the lord hath set you free and brought you into joy, then you think you have overcome all, but there is a daily Cross to be taken up while the fleshly will remaineth. . . . [L]ooking out to satisfy the will of the flesh, there doth the Serpent get in & tells the Creature of ease, & liberty in the flesh, and say thou needest to take up the Cross no longer, for thou art now come to thy rest, thou may eat & drink and be merry & I will give thee joy enough & thus many a poor soul is drowned and runs on in lightness & wantonness . . . . O dear friends beware & exhort others, that we may sit down in the lowest room, taking up the Cross daily and following Christ and that he may go before us & lead us at his one pleasure. I have experience of the wiles of Satan, the lord hath exercised me, but there is no way but sit down and submit to his will & there is rest and peace.[183]*

Again and again, after being "exercised" by this inner struggle, Elizabeth Hooton surrendered to the inward prompting of Christ. In 1652 she joined George Fox and others traveling in York. For interrupting a service in a church at Rotherham, she was imprisoned in York Castle's dungeon for sixteen months. Later, she twice made the long journey to Puritan New England. In the colony of Massachusetts, she was stripped to the waist and whipped repeatedly. Several times she was left to die in a snowy wilderness along the border with Rhode Island. She survived and returned again and again to speak and witness in Massachusetts, in spite of the brutal punishments inflicted on her.

An inward death of what early Friends called "the first man," which has a fallen nature, is necessary before the "new man," restored in the original pure human condition, can be restored or reborn. Living in the cross makes this death and rebirth possible. As the first Friends discovered, over time the faithful learn to give over their will to divine direction in more and more areas of life, and Christ comes to be fully formed within. In the cross, one gives up all attitudes and behaviors that don't originate in God's Love. This self-denial is necessary in order that Christ may be "all" in each person.

Francis Howgill explained how one must learn not to act from the impulses of the self-will, but instead to let God and Christ be the active force within. What the inward Christ wants to do with your life is often not the same as what you have wanted for yourself. The will of God for Howgill was that he leave his family to travel in the ministry for decades, teaching others how to find Christ within. In addition to traveling and speaking, Howgill wrote many documents, some in languages other than his native tongue. He spent time in prison early in his ministry and again during the final five years of his life. He explained the difference between following one's own ideas of what God wants and actually letting God be the initiator and active principle:

It is not your good words, without the life of godliness, nor your swelling speeches, that are accepted with God; for he accepts nothing except that which is of himself, and by him wrought in the creature by his own will and power. . . . This work, which he works of himself, and by his power, and in his covenant, is perfect, and is accepted of God. Therefore, it is no longer the creature but Christ, who is all in his saints. . . . The covenant of life is made manifest! Glory to him in the highest! . . . Self must be denied . . . that he [Christ] may be all and you nothing. He gives freely, and his gift is perfect and pure. . . . And this grace has separated me from sin, and has constrained me to deny myself, and follow him through the death of the cross, and through the denial of all, both country and nation, kindred, and tongues, and people, and from wife and children and houses and lands, to publish his name abroad contrary to my own will, and to make known to you the riches of his grace, which all who wait in the light of Christ Jesus will come to see.[184]

The Cross in Our Time

Mistaken understandings of the crucifixion have contributed to an institutional form of Christianity that has long denied the sanctity of the body, the planet, and life on earth. Those with power—whether political or religious— have sometimes misused the concept of the cross to manipulate people into submission or unhealthy self-denial. In many times and places, oppressed people have been taught not to resist oppression but to passively accept their suffering as God's will. Given this history, does the concept of "living in the cross" still have meaning?

The abuses of the past make it difficult for some to understand the spiritual significance of the cross. For many Friends today, however, the cross is still a powerful symbol of the suffering and self-denial Jesus accepted as part of the cost of bringing God's love and forgiveness. Jesus did not want to be crucified, but he was willing to surrender his own will, and he carried out a ministry that led to the cross. For Quakers today, to "live in the cross" is to make sacrifices that our limited human will would prefer not to make, and to do so for the sake of God's greater purposes. Each time we make a sacrifice that God is calling us to make, a human part of ourselves, sometimes called the self-will or the ego, loses some of its control. This allows the Seed of God to grow and become the stronger principle within. Making sacrifices that God is not calling for, however, is a way of strengthening our self-will, not a way of becoming closer to God. Ongoing, careful discernment is, therefore, necessary. Gradually, we learn to surrender completely to the divine way in all things. Although this requires sacrifice and sometimes leads to suffering, eventually we discover the joy and spiritual freedom that come from living in union with God. Eventually, we discover that the desires that had to be denied were not the deepest, truest desires of our souls.

Parenting is a way many people surrender their own wills. Raising children reveals to parents behaviors and motivations in themselves that are not meeting their standards of truth and love; this is part of the Refiner's Fire. Raising children also involves a profound experience of living in the cross. Parents daily sacrifice their time, energy, comforts, and preferences in order to nurture and support their children. They also suffer when their children experience misfortunes, make mistakes, or follow different paths than the parents would have chosen.

Arthur O. Roberts adhered wholeheartedly to the Quaker peace testimony against fighting in outward wars. He was distressed, therefore, when his son entered military service during the Vietnam War, serving for four years on a nuclear submarine. His daughters also challenged their parents. In his autobiography, Roberts describes the anguish he and his wife, Fern, endured over some of the choices their children made: "[We] suffered sleepless nights, agonizing in prayer over our children. Our own needs became hostage to our children, our own affection mortgaged to their wills, or so it seemed."[185] Their despair for their children was a form of living in the cross. From this experience, they learned patience, forgiveness, and many other lessons.

> *We learned never to give up on each other, and that love never fails. From family experiences we came to understand more about the Cross, about how generously God forgives, about human limits and the power of truth and love. We became less legalistic and more compassionate, but not without much agony of spirit. Familial love can rise above differing convictions and interests, we discovered. Moral judgment is not compromised by God's mercy, God's grace covers us all.*[186]

Tensions between the generations gradually dissolved. A deeper love and understanding resulted. Later, while participating in military exercises on the China Sea, the Roberts' son became convinced that he "could never fire MIRV nuclear missiles at an enemy city,"[187] and he left military service.

Each day, opportunities arise to choose God's will. We "live in the cross" whenever we respond to God's leading to offer service or sacrifice to someone in need of assistance. In the course of family and work life, there are always invitations to choose the way of peace, love, and truth even when our emotions, fears, or ego want to direct us differently. Following a leading of any sort generally requires some aspect of self-control, self-denial, or challenge that invites us to "die to ourselves" and live into the ways of God and Christ. Leadings ask us to give our energy and resources to God's projects rather than those of our own devising. We are asked to give time we might have preferred to spend in comfortable or pleasurable pastimes with family and friends. Damaris Mercedes Guardado Lemus of El Salvador was young when she began accompanying evangelical medical brigades in rural areas as an interpreter. Since then, her call to ministry has slowly grown. To respond faithfully has required sacrifice:

> *It's important to mention that as a young person this business of being called causes a lot of fear because we don't feel prepared and above all we don't want to give up the secular life—as you sacrifice beautiful moments with your family, the salary that a job could generate, or the comfort and pleasantness of having time to do nothing. This is about making decisions, and as young people we can only make good decisions under the guidance of our Lord. Faith takes the place of security when it is time to make decisions.[188]*

Gladys Kang'ahi, who has traveled widely in the ministry, offers some queries that help people with a similar call to consider the difficult challenge of being asked to surrender to God's ways:

> *Do you have the wisdom and the heart to repent of all the things that might obstruct your service? Do you have the heart to forgive even the unforgivable? Do you have what it takes to love the unlovable, to walk and talk with those you think are your enemies? Will you be able to see everyone as belonging to the community of God and not otherwise?[189]*

We experience the cross whenever we are led to do something that is contrary to our personal preferences, anything that challenges us to confront our fears, prejudices, and discomfort. In 1990, Buffalo (New York) Meeting asked the new task group on Friends in Unity with Nature to create a program for the twentieth anniversary of Earth Day. After Steven Davison and a friend prayed about how to do this, Davison received an opening that "would not go away." He shared it with others, but it was not well received. Nonetheless, it continued to develop. He wrote:

And in a few weeks, the opening had become a leading to write a book about earth stewardship based on a radical reading of the Bible. Now I had spent the last several years persecuting Christians in my meeting and actively opposing teaching the Bible in First Day School. I hated the Bible. But once, I had loved the Bible. And I knew it really well. . . . This leading was what Friends used to call a "cross to the will," meaning that my own will would have to be crucified in order to be faithful. . . . The leading led me back to the Bible. I have been studying it lovingly ever since. The way I knew it was a leading from God was that it grew so organically, it was a cross to the will, and it bore such abundant fruit—and I could not not follow it.[190]

Those following a leading will often encounter resistance from others. When the resistance comes from members of one's own community, it is important to humbly listen to the reasons for it and to discern about the leading with one's community. Sometimes objections to someone's sense of leading are prompted by the Spirit and are a God-given test to clarify or refine the leading. Sometimes, however, objections arise from other motives, including fear or envy. In such cases, enduring resistance or obstacles and persevering is part of living in the cross. Facing and overcoming obstacles builds patience, endurance, and faith. Priscilla Makhino's call to ministry has led her to travel widely beyond her home in Africa. To do this, she has received much support from her family and Quaker community. She has also experienced many obstacles, some from members of her own community. She takes heart from the Beatitudes and has learned that if she perseveres with faith and prayer, the way becomes clear: "Stops and offenses have many, many times come my way, but they have always become stepping-stones for me."[191]

Over time, living in the cross teaches us to let go of whatever impedes the work of God in and through us. We learn to choose the path of peace even when we are angry, to be truthful when we would rather hide in silence or deception, to be loving when we feel selfish. Ultimately, we must also release any form of identity that is not given to us by God. During his 2013 Swarthmore lecture, Gerald Hewitson described the deeply negative messages about himself he had accepted in childhood. Years of inner work in the Light allowed him to "relinquish fear, guilt, anger, and a sense of control." After many years of spiritual growth, he then experienced "going to the cross." This led to the death of a false sense of self:

> There came a point during, in what for me was a lengthy process, when I found myself completely rewriting . . . my internal life narrative, of who I was, and how I needed to respond to the world. . . . These understandings were not the work of a moment, but a long slow process of realization, recognition, and fumbling attempts to live out a new reality. But they started with a blinding moment of recognition. This experience felt like being in a blast furnace, where the quite ordinary elements of stone and ore are transformed into steel in a furnace of white heat. It was intense, powerful, physical: it felt like excruciating agony. When dealing with emotional pain the secular world is fond of bland phrases, with the force and energy removed from them: phrases like moving on, letting things go. We rarely get to words like laying down or relinquishing, let alone sacrifice. The first Quakers had the exact phrase for my experience: going to the cross. This is not a term the modern ear likes to hear. Yet it describes the experience of Quakers over many generations. We go to the cross when we sacrifice the person we think we might be, should be or would like to be for the person we are intended to be. It is a coming home to that person we truly are.[192]

Hewitson discovered that the death of his old sense of self was necessary for the transformation God wanted to work in him: to birth into being the person he was created to be. He counsels Friends,

> *We can remember that the crucifixion is not a story of extinction, but one of complete transformation; not death, but release into a state beyond the world's comprehension. In this process we release those energies deep within ourselves, energies hidden from us in the habits of our usual daily existence. . . . This was all part of my internal reworking.*[193]

Living in the cross is about not being controlled by our baser instincts and desires. It is about dying to a false self and being born to a new self. It is also about participating in God's work of transforming the world. In varied ways, we are called to help address the fear, greed, and ignorance that prevails in the world and to work for a society based on compassion, justice, and mutual trust. Over the centuries, Quakers have found God leading them to make bold statements and take risky actions for the sake of incarnating God's kingdom more fully on earth. Following Philippians 2:5–8, Christian theology has long pointed out that Jesus was a model of *kenosis*, sacrificing or emptying himself for the sake of others:

> *Let the same mind be in you that was in Christ Jesus, who, though he was in the form of God, did not regard equality with God as something to be exploited, but emptied himself, taking the form of a slave, being born in human likeness. And being found in human form, he humbled himself and became obedient to the point of death—even death on a cross.*

Cosmologist and professor of applied mathematics George Ellis, a member of a South African Quaker meeting, has posited that "*kenosis* is the underlying [ethical] law of the

133

universe."[194] He witnessed this in his own life when he and his meeting participated in work to end apartheid, work that often seemed on the brink of failure yet ultimately resulted in his country's remarkable change to a more just government.

Starting in the late 1940s, African American Quaker Bayard Rustin was a leader in the movement to combat racism in the United States. His lifelong efforts powerfully demonstrated how living in the cross can transform society, moving it toward God's desires for justice and equality. Rustin's Quaker grandmother, with whom he lived as a child, was one of the founders of the National Association for the Advancement of Colored People, and NAACP leaders such as W. E. B. Du Bois visited their home when Rustin was a child. In his newly integrated high school, Rustin inspired fellow teammates to protest his exclusion from a restaurant. While incarcerated in segregated federal penitentiaries, Rustin joined a hunger strike and in other ways protested the harsh treatment of black prisoners. Only on Sundays was he allowed to visit his white friends in the upper floors. When a prisoner opposed to the mixing of the races beat him with a stick, Rustin told his friends not to intervene. The man continued hitting him until the stick shattered. Then he stopped, shaking, unable to continue beating someone who was not hitting back.

It is powerful when a single individual accepts living in the cross. Over time, the change in one individual transforms people and situations around them. It is far more powerful, however, when groups hear this call and live according to God's way of love, even in the face of resistance or persecution. After release from prison, Rustin traveled to India to meet and learn from those who had worked with Mahatma Gandhi. In the 1940s, under Gandhi's spiritual leadership, India had won liberation from British Rule through steadfast nonviolent resistance. Sometimes Gandhian protestors endured harsh physical punishment. The world's outrage at British brutality against nonviolent protestors helped India gain liberation.

Rustin was led to apply such lessons to liberating black Americans from systemic racism. He worked for the American Friends Service Committee, teaching pacifism, and then worked for the Fellowship of Reconciliation, an ecumenical Christian peace and civil rights organization. Rustin helped organize the Fellowship of Reconciliation's 1947 Freedom Ride. Called the Journey of Reconciliation, it was designed to draw attention to the 1946 U.S. Supreme Court ruling that segregation on public interstate buses was unconstitutional. Sixteen men participated, eight of them black and eight white. All of them were willing to sacrifice and suffer, if necessary, in order to help end racial oppression in the United States. These Freedom Riders rode Southern interstate buses in pairs, one white man and one black man sitting together in sections reserved for whites only or blacks only. They were illegally harassed, and some were beaten and arrested. Rustin and two white colleagues were sentenced to labor on a chain gang in North Carolina. They were chained together with others every day as they labored under the hot sun. Released after twenty-two days of harsh and humiliating conditions, Rustin wrote a six-part series that was published in the *New York Post* under the title "22 Days on a Chain Gang." The resulting public outcry soon led to the abolition of chain gangs in North Carolina.

Rustin co-founded the Southern Christian Leadership Conference with Martin Luther King Jr. and other faith-based leaders. He brought a great deal of wisdom and experience to the Civil Rights Movement of the 1960s. When King hired armed guards and obtained a gun after his home was bombed, Rustin rushed to the house and reminded the younger man that a nonviolent movement has more spiritual and moral power than a violent one, even though it means being vulnerable. In the years that followed, it was the nonviolence of civil rights advocates, even in the face of brutality, that appealed to the conscience of their fellow Americans. This ultimately led to the passage of new civil rights laws.

Drawing on decades of experience planning marches and demonstrations, Rustin was the prime organizer of the 1963 March on Washington for Jobs and Freedom, which drew more than 250,000 participants of all races and was the largest demonstration in the nation's capital up to that time. However, other civil rights leaders kept Rustin's role in the background because he was a gay man.

We have seen examples of people in our times who have made various kinds of sacrifices in order to serve God's larger, loving purposes. Does God ever lead Friends today into laying down their lives? Tom Fox of Langley Hill Friends Meeting in Virginia showed that sometimes this is so. Fox believed that the way to take part in the creation of the "Peaceable Realm of God" is to follow the two commandments Jesus named as most important, namely, to "love God with all our heart, our mind and our strength and to love our neighbors and enemies as we love God and ourselves."[195] During the Vietnam War, Fox's conscience did not allow him to engage in killing. Instead, he joined the United States Marine Band as a clarinet player. Later, while working as an assistant manager at a Whole Foods store, he was a beloved adult presence at Quaker youth gatherings, serving as a mentor to teenagers.

When terrorists flew airplanes into buildings in New York City and Washington, D.C., on September 11, 2001, killing about 3,000 people, outraged U.S. citizens urged their country toward violent retaliation. Some Americans threatened or committed violence against fellow citizens who were Muslim, and the United States initiated wars in Afghanistan and then Iraq, causing the deaths of at least 100,000 and possibly half a million or more civilians in those countries.[196] Tom Fox felt called to "find some way to pull us out of the darkness and move the world (even if it was the movement of one human being) towards the light."[197] In 2004, he joined Christian Peacemaker Teams (CPT) and its peace work in Palestine and Iraq. Fully cognizant of the risk involved, Fox and his fellow CPT members lived and worked in a typical Baghdad neighborhood, among ordinary Iraqis, serving as a peaceful presence and intermediary between Iraqis in prison and their families. Fox was friendly to both the U.S. occupiers and the local people. He was one of four CPT members who were taken hostage in Iraq in 2005 and was the only U.S. citizen among them. Four months later, his captors killed him. After their rescue, his fellow hostages told of ways that Fox had continued to love his neighbors and his enemies even in captivity.

Many saw Tom Fox's gentle service and ultimate sacrifice as evidence of how God's love is active in the world. Peggy Senger Morrison wrote about Fox as follows: "He was a man changed by timeless truth, and being changed himself, he changed the world around him. Not content to just know the truth, he acted upon it."[198] In her view, Fox voluntarily gave his life in God's service:

> *Tom Fox laid his life down a long time ago. He surrendered it into the hands of the Divine. Because he knew it was safe there, he was able to walk unbound by fear, letting the Light within him control and impel him forward into the work of peace. Tom's life was safe in the hands of God before he went to Baghdad, it was safe in Baghdad, it was safe in captivity, and it is safe now.*[199]

God's leadings sometimes take people into forms of service and ministry that involve suffering. However, it can be difficult to discern whether God is really calling us to live in the cross in such a way. Many impulses toward self-sacrifice are not divine but come from the ego, social conditioning, or faulty interpretations of religion. People may imagine that something is a way of "living in the cross" when it is actually contrary to God's desires. Guilt or fear prompt many to conform to oppression or to sacrifice their well-being. Sacrifices motivated not by divine leadings but by something else can actually strengthen the ego and make it more difficult to hear God's will. Thus, when a person feels impelled to undertake a task, action, or lifestyle choice that could have painful consequences, it is vitally important to seek help in discerning if this is actually a spiritual leading from God or if it is motivated by other impulses.

After experiencing illness, painful diminishments, or losses, some Friends reconsider whether or not they have actually been following God in making self-sacrificing choices. One Friend worked for years in a job in which she was expected to do more than one person is able to do and remain healthy. After suffering from serious illness, she wrote,

> I struggle a great deal [with] the way in which my inner "should" messages are so strong that I mix them up with God's voice. I am convinced that, through thinking that I must push myself hard in order to be faithful to God, (and for many years doing so), I have diminished my resilience, perhaps contributing to [my illness]. Thinking about "the cross" is confusing because it reinforces that kind of self-driving tendency, which I formerly thought was obedience but now question. . . . So, faithfulness is not a settled matter for me, but I think that it means something very different than I have previously understood. Jesus spoke of bringing abundance, and that is more where I feel life.[200]

For early Quakers, as well as Friends today, a sense of Life, as well as of God's love and power, have been important signs of the presence of God in a leading. To be faithful, we must *only* accept the cross to our wills that God gives us, not one that we devise for ourselves, not one forced on us by society, not one urged by family or culture. The death of the false self that comes eventually as the result of surrender to God's will is, paradoxically, a death that leads to a greater, more abundant life, a life lived in the love and power of the Light.

138

Conservative Friend Bill Taber often spoke of "the cross of joy," which referred to his experience of discovering joy after surrendering to God's will against his own preferences. The next element of the Quaker spiritual journey, abiding, speaks of the divine Love and spiritual power that can pour into the emptied space in those who live in the cross.

Reflection Questions

The Cross

Has being faithful led you into an experience of suffering or sacrifice, or what early Friends spoke of as a "cross" to your own will? What happened? What did you learn from that?

How do you struggle when led to do something that is uncomfortable or risky?

What struggles do you have with the concept or practice of "living in the cross"?

Have you ever discovered that you were making sacrifices that were not leadings from God but were prompted by other motivations?

Have you ever found peace when surrendering your personal will to follow God's will? Has spiritual joy or power been given you to help you follow a difficult leading?

Has following your leadings and attempting daily faithfulness changed you or your sense of who you really are?

Abiding in the Seventeenth Century

Abide in me as I abide in you. . . . As the Father
has loved me, so I have loved you; abide in my
love. If you keep my commandments, you will
abide in my love, just as I have kept my Father's
commandments and abide in his love.

—John 15:4, 9–10

In surrendering to the Light of Christ Within, the first Quakers acquiesced to a process of profound transformation. It was a difficult journey, made possible by the spiritual power that flowed into them and by a community that was knitted together and sustained by God's Love. Writings by early Friends speak frequently of the spiritual power found in the Quaker movement when it began. Wealthy Isaac and Mary Penington were reluctant to publicly join with Friends because it would require many sacrifices. However, Mary admired the Quakers she met who had "power over their corruptions." They were able to stop participating in deceptive and ultimately oppressive social norms because of the spiritual power that was active in them. She wanted to be empowered by God in that way, too. Once the Peningtons found the faith and courage to become Quakers in a public way, they felt free to invite other Friends to worship with them in their own home. For Mary Penington, this was an entrance into God's Love and Joy that was all that she had prayed for:

Oh! the joy that filled my soul in the first meeting
ever held in our house at Chalfont. To this day, I
have a fresh remembrance of it. It was then the
Lord enabled me to worship him in that which was
undoubtedly his own, and give up my whole
strength, yea to swim in the life which overcame
me that day. Oh! Long had I desired to worship
him with acceptation, and lift up my hands
without doubting, which I witnessed that day in

141

*that assembly. I acknowledged his great mercy
and wonderful kindness, for I could say, "This is it
which I have longed and waited for, and feared I
never should have experienced.*[201]

A felt experience of God's Power characterized gatherings
of the first Friends, who often wrote, "The Power of the Lord
was over all." This power gave them the courage to make the
changes God required. As people learned to surrender to the
Refiner's Fire and felt how it freed them for the new life for
which they had been longing, they understood that the
process of purification, however challenging, was a form of
divine Love. They learned to follow God's guidance in more
and more aspects of their lives, thereby learning to abide in
God's Power and not depart from it.

After William Dewsbury became convinced that the
Quaker movement was inspired and guided by God,
spiritual power enabled him to endure conditions of great
physical misery with a calm and happy heart, including
many long imprisonments:

*I never since played the coward; but joyfully
entered prisons as palaces, telling mine enemies to
hold me there as long as they could. And in the
prison-house, I sang praises to my God, and
esteemed the bolts and locks put upon me as
jewels; and in the name of the eternal God I
always got the victory. For they could keep me no
longer than the determined time of my God.*[202]

Deeply heart-opening, bonding experiences of love also
characterized the beginning of Quakerism. It was during the
silence of gathered meetings that many early Friends had
their first awesome experience of being tangibly immersed
in divine Love. When Francis Howgill described entire
groups being caught up, as by a net, into the kingdom of
heaven, he emphasized how they became bound together
in love. "And from that day forward," he wrote, "our hearts
were knit unto the Lord and one unto another in true and
fervent love, in the covenant of Life with God."[203] John

Banks, too, wrote about being bonded with others through the experience in worship:

> And Oh! the days and nights of comfort and divine consolation we were made partakers of in those days together (and the faithful and true of heart still are). And in the same inward sense, and feeling of the Lord's power and presence, we enjoyed one another, and were near and dear one unto another.[204]

When they persisted in faithfulness even through difficulties, Friends' hearts become enlarged with spiritual love not only for members of their own community but for others as well. Many experienced love for particular people who were suffering or in spiritual need to whom they were drawn to bring God's Truth and loving ministry. As they allowed divine Love to move inside, it began to flow through them, and they learned to abide in that love.

Early Quakers frequently described having the divine Fountain of Love flowing into and through them. Traveling minister Ambrose Rigge began a eulogy with the words,

> The Spirit of the Lord is upon me, and the fountain of love and life is open in my soul, and freely floweth towards all my dear brethren and fellow labourers in the great harvest of our Lord and Master.[205]

James Nayler advised Friends to

> meet often together in the spirit and power of the Lord Jesus Christ, and therein mind to be gathered into the fountain of love and knowledge, that therein you may love one another, and from thence send forth love to all the creation, which now in love he is visiting.[206]

For many, the divine Fountain of Love was more than an idea; it was a tangible experience.

Communities and networks of Friends found themselves bound together in love for one another. Those who served as mentors by preaching, teaching, and modeling the Quaker message were like spiritual mothers and fathers. A tender love infused relationships between those who traveled and suffered in the ministry together. Letters the traveling ministers wrote to each other show that they were carried through their difficult trials by a strong feeling of being enfolded by God's Love and an awareness of being bonded in love to one another. Marmaduke Stevenson and Christopher Holder traveled together in the harsh territory of New England and were frequently imprisoned. During a period when Holder was incarcerated in Boston and Stevenson was at liberty, Stevenson wrote the following to console his imprisoned companion:

O my dearly beloved of my father, my soul and life salutes thee, for thou are dear to me in the love which changeth not, but doth endure forever; am I one with thee in the life and power of truth, where we are joined together as members of his Body who is our Head, and our preserver night and day, where we are kept safe under the shadow of his wings, where we feed together in the green pastures by the pleasant springs, where thou may feel me, my beloved one, at the living fountain which doth refresh the whole city of our God, where we are daily refreshed together in the banqueting house, where we do receive strength and nourishment from him who is our life and fills us with his living virtue day by day, which is as precious ointment poured forth giving a pleasant smell, and is pleasant to behold. For it hath ravished our hearts whereby we are constrained to leave all to follow it, who gathers our hearts in one, where I am joined and sealed with thee in the covenant of life.[207]

Divinely inspired love helped Friends risk and endure incredible punishments for the sake of helping others know

God and live in the Light. Those called to travel in the ministry were motivated by God's love for the divine Seed, Christ, in those to whom they were sent. In a tract detailing the numerous life-threatening punishments she endured in the course of her ministry in Puritan Massachusetts, Elizabeth Hooton wrote,

> All this and much more I have gone through and suffered, and much more could I for the Seed's sake which is Buried and Oppressed. . . . Yes, the Love that I bear to the Souls of all Men, making me willing to undergo whatsoever can be inflicted.[208]

After her yearlong journey to bring a message to the sultan of Turkey, Mary Fisher wrote of the powerful love engendered in her heart for the people of Turkey:

> They are more near truth than many Nations. There is a love begot in me towards them which is endless, but this is my hope concerning them, that he who hath raised me to love them more than many others will also raise his seed in them unto which my love is. Nevertheless, though they be called Turks, the seed of them is near unto God, and their kindness hath in some measure been shown to his servants.[209]

Many early Friends who made sacrifices and suffered as a result of carrying out God's leadings had deeply consoling experiences of heavenly love, accompanied by an awareness of God's overriding, ultimate power. Barbara Blaugdone, for example, recounts numerous experiences when divine Love and Power enabled her to be faithful in hardship. During moments of physical attack, the love that filled her subsumed her fear and physical pain:

> As Mary Prince and I was coming Arm in Arm from a Meeting, that was at George Bishop's House, there was a Rude Man came and abused us, and struck off Mary Prince her Hat, and run some sharp Knife or Instrument through all my

145

Clothes, into the side of my Belly, which if it had gone a little farther, it might have killed me; but my Soul was so in love with the Truth, that I could have given up my Life for it at that day.

[In Exeter Prison] the Sheriff came with a Beadle [a messenger of a law court], *and had me into a Room, and Whipt me till the Blood ran down my Back, and I never startled at a blow; but the Lord made me to rejoyce, that I was counted Worthy to Suffer for his Name's sake, and I Sung aloud; and the Beadle said, Do ye Sing; I shall make ye Cry by and by: and with that he laid more Stripes, and laid them on very hard. I shall never forget the large Experience of the Love and Power of God which I had in my Travels, and therefore I can speak to his Praise, and glorifie his Name: for if he had Whipt me to Death in that state which then I was in, I should not have been terrified and dismayed at it; Ann Speed was an Eye Witness of it, and she stood and lookt in at the Window, and wept bitterly.*[210]

Condemned to hang in Boston, Marmaduke Stevenson, William Robinson, and Mary Dyer walked to the gallows hand in hand. Although they were surrounded by armed men beating drums, they were calm, filled with a peaceful assurance. One official asked Mary Dyer, a middle-aged mother of many children, if she wasn't ashamed to be holding the hands of two young men. She responded that she was immersed in the flow of divine Love, upheld by God:

This is to me an hour of the greatest joy I ever had in this World. No ear can hear, no tongue can utter, no heart can understand the sweet incomes or influence, and the refreshings of the Spirit of the Lord which now I feel.[211]

Abiding in Our Time

Engaging in spiritual practices on a regular basis, over time, helps Friends to learn how to abide in God's Love, Peace, and Power. Bill Taber, a longtime teacher of Quakerism at Pendle Hill, describes how entering into the divine Presence can be a tangible experience in meeting for worship:

> *Entering into worship often feels to me somewhat like entering into a stream, which, though invisible to our outward eye, feels just as real as does a stream of water when we step into it. Just as bathing in a real stream of pure flowing water needs no justification to one who has experienced the vitality it brings, so entering into the stream of worship needs no justification to one who has experienced the healing, the peace, the renewal, the expansion which accompanies this altered state of consciousness. I once thought worship was something I do, but for many years now it has seemed as if worship is actually a state of consciousness which I enter, so that I am immersed into a living, invisible stream of reality which has always been present throughout all history. In some mysterious way this stream unites me with the communion of the saints across the ages and brings me into the presence of the Living Christ, the Word, the Logos written of in the Gospel of John.*[212]

In his Pendle Hill pamphlet *Four Doors to Meeting for Worship*, Taber gives guidance not only about how to enter into that living stream during a period of worship, but also suggests daily practices that can help Friends learn to enter that "altered state of communal consciousness" at any time, day or night. Like many Friends before him, he recommends taking a period of "daily retirement" from the outward activity and business of one's life. During such a daily period, Friends contemplate a passage of the Bible, rest silently "in the eternal arms," meditate, appreciate beauty, or pray for themselves and others. Taber also recommends sharing with spiritual friends about our life with God and taking time with these Friends for spontaneous opportunities to worship together. Such practices help us to "re-awaken to our rich inborn capacity to be alive to the spiritual dimension."[213] They help us abide in the living Presence during the activities of our days, even while engaging in conversation or going about our work.

Another way that Friends learn to abide in the divine Presence is to have faith in divine providence, to trust that God will provide the outward means to support faithful response to the movements of the Spirit. This can happen through the coming together of inward and outward events in ways that are sometimes described as "synchronicity." Quakers speak of "way opening" when God leads them into ministry or action. As a counselor at Catoctin Quaker Camp, Rob Jones practiced trusting in the unfolding of God's providence while leading groups on hiking trips lasting several days. They would set a destination but not the route and then let an adventure unfold. One day, as a heavy rain was about to fall without any obvious shelter in sight, Jones and his fellow counselor reminded themselves that "way opens." Moments later, a driver stopped and invited the group to sleep on her screened porch that night, out of the rain. Later, she also cooked dinner for them. Such experiences taught Jones to act in trust that "if we put one foot in front of the other and start toward something that the next steps will become clear, the way will open."[214]

In a faltering global economy, when many young people are not finding stable employment, Jones has been helping others live with uncertainty in a spirit of trust. After finishing graduate school, he decided not to obtain a regular job. Instead, he has engaged in an unconventional enterprise, building a local food system in the Triangle region of North Carolina. In 2010 *New York Times Magazine* published a feature article about Crop Mob, started by Jones as a way for young people interested in farming to gather in groups of forty or fifty and work for several hours helping small farmers with big projects, providing a great deal of inexpensive labor to the farmers in a short time and a powerful experience of community to the young people.[215] Jones has learned it is possible to live a full life without holding onto middle-class forms of stability:

> I've lived rent free in my tent, house sitting, in a bunk house, and now in a yurt. I'm living simply and sipping on my savings while I build a new kind of capital. I don't measure my success by the amount of money I earn, which is virtually none, but by the relationships I'm building, the community that is forming, and by the good local food that I eat.[216]

Jones writes that he is at peace with uncertainty: "All I want to be saying at the end of the day is 'Way opens,' and it will."[217]

Experiences of God's loving, empowering Presence and guidance have transformed the lives of many Friends in our time who are learning how to abide in that presence. Peggy Senger Morrison tells numerous stories about being guided and protected by divine Power, especially when traveling in the ministry. She experiences this even while riding her motorcycle in unknown terrain, or perhaps especially then. By facing many difficulties and dangers, and through finding grace and help along the way, she has come to trust in the power that comes from abiding in Christ's love:

> I came to understand His protection as the state of being, in which, surrounded by His love, other things, including some pretty major hurts, begin to heal and rapidly lose their power over me. Some things that ought to hurt don't even bother me anymore. His Love has become my armor.[218]

Richard Taylor, a longtime Quaker activist, describes many risks taken in order to witness for justice and take a stand for equality in the face of violence and threats. During times of public witness, he learned to pray continually. He and his companions also took time to listen for guidance step by step. Abiding in God and Christ in this way gave him the courage to act, sometimes even lifting him up in situations of danger. For example, Taylor, his wife, and several others paddled canoes and kayaks to block the freighter *Padma* from docking in Baltimore Harbor to collect weapons that the U.S. government was secretly shipping to East Pakistan. Their action drew media attention to what the government was doing. The Taylors were also part of a group that marched in Selma during the Civil Rights Movement. At critical moments, the Spirit provided Taylor just the words he needed to speak.

During the Vietnam War, Taylor and several others were arrested for blocking a train carrying weapons of war. When a judge asked him to make a statement, Taylor remembered the story of Jesus telling his disciples that the Spirit would provide the words to say in times of trial. When it was his turn to speak, Taylor experienced the truth of this:

> And indeed, when the judge called me to make a statement, it seemed as though the courtroom, the other defendants, the court officials, and observers just fell away, leaving a sort of "path" of vibrating light between me and the judge. My words seemed to flow out effortlessly. It seemed that the Spirit which Jesus promised was there.[219]

Those who learn to abide in God's Love sometimes have the experience that they are living in two levels of reality simultaneously, interacting in daily events and at the same time abiding with God in their center, aware of a spiritual reality that undergirds everything. As Thomas Kelly wrote:

> There is a way of ordering our mental life on more than one level at once. On one level we may be thinking, discussing, seeing, calculating, meeting all the demands of external affairs. But deep within, behind the scenes, at a profounder level, we may also be in prayer and adoration,

song and worship and a gentle receptiveness to divine breathings.[220]

When Priscilla Makhino travels far from home in the ministry to which God has called her, she feels extra spiritual support surrounding her. She writes, "In hard places and during attacks of sadness, I feel angels hovering around in a very special way." In difficult situations, she sometimes has dreams or visions, like the ones that healed her long ago, in which people are ministering to her. She wakes healed, her mind sound.[221] More than this, she feels guidance and spiritual power coming from Christ. "While I travel," she writes, "I always hear His voice and feel His presence every hour."[222] While attending a triennial session of the Friends World Committee for Consultation, which brings together Friends from all the continents on which there are Quakers, Makhino felt that God was powerfully present. She was led to get on her knees and pray for the gathering for four hours. Every day she felt God giving her words to speak, and she also felt power coming through her when she prayed for several sick people.

Spiritual experiences, both during meetings for worship and in daily life, teach Friends to trust in God's Love and healing power. Philadelphia Yearly Meeting's gatherings for "extended worship" include a full morning of unprogrammed worship that lasts about three hours. Often these are gathered meetings, in which many feel a special sense of God's Presence and activity. Soon after the tragic events of September 11, 2001, Louise Mullen arrived at one of these gatherings bent over from pain in her back. During the meeting for worship she was lifted out of this pain by an experience of God's immense love:

> *I was sharply aware of the pain and at one point began to move forward on the bench to get relief. I thought the move was intentional, then realized that in the most gentle, tender and strong way I was being moved. I was experiencing the great flowing energy of the Divine. At first I thought*

this could be a call to speak, but there were no words accompanying the power I felt. After a while I opened my eyes, looked around at the precious souls and knew that the same powerful love I felt in my body had permeated the entire room and all the people it held. I don't know how long I bathed in this awareness of the Great Love, feeling no pain in my body. When worship came to a close, I rose from the bench with a knowing, once again, of God's presence, as well as the depth and vastness of the power of that love which is inextinguishable. [223]

After that gathering, Mullen returned to this experience many times since, finding,

comfort . . . in knowing that this indescribable power of life is eternal, and it is only this which can sustain and bring peace to these chaotic times. As I do what I can in peace-making activities, this knowing in my heart is what I carry with me. [224]

Powerful openings to God's Love often draw people into a deeper ongoing closeness to God, allowing them to abide in that love in both the ordinary experiences of life and during life's biggest challenges. After Helene Pollock's life was transformed by a powerful opening, she became committed to focusing her life on God and learning to draw on divine Love and Power to be more courageous:

In the months and years following that special night, fragmented pieces of my life came together under the umbrella of God's love, and I changed a lot. Much of this was due to daily prayer. Of course, I still made many mistakes, but the main change is that I became much more of a risk-taker. I became increasingly aware of God's Truth and able to speak truth to power. So I was more confident in facing challenges at work, in my Meeting and in my friendships. When I was diagnosed with an aggressive form

of breast cancer, I was at peace, trusting God
each step of the way.[225]

Michael Resman spent his career as an occupational therapist working with disabled children and gave his free time to help build homes for Habitat for Humanity. He discovered that "to love God completely is to lose control of one's life." After crippling arthritis in his hands made him unable to do the kind of work he had been doing, he felt led to increase the time he spent every day in prayer. This invisible ministry of prayer serves the world in ways he glimpses from time to time. He has discovered that paying attention to God allows three gifts to flow toward us: spiritual joy, serenity, and brief experiences of heaven on earth, gifts that sometimes seem to be related, he says, to "how wisely I'm conducting myself."

The first gift, spiritual joy,

> *is different from the exuberant happiness on the*
> *faces of the winning team's fans. Spiritual joy*
> *comes from knowing God loves us. . . . I can be ill,*
> *hurting, grieving or fearful—and yet joyful under*
> *those feelings because God loves me.*[226]

Serenity, the second gift, comes from experiencing God's forgiveness and the resultant freedom from the fears that infect so many.

"Yes, I will know illness, loss, failures and rejection," Resman writes. "All that pales in relation to the fact that God will always love me." Although he often feels spiritual joy and serenity, he has occasionally experienced what he calls "heaven on earth," moments of feeling connected both to God and to everything on earth. In those moments, he knows that

> *all is well, because I am right with God. I know*
> *joy, bliss and peace. What a blessing to be so*
> *aware of God's presence. This happens when my*
> *will is perfectly aligned with God's. I want*
> *nothing other than what God wants.*[227]

These experiences are rare. Resman continues to seek to abide always in God's will, making himself available to serve God's leadings, big and small.

During the six months that Linda Caldwell Lee spent alone in a relative's beach house recovering from illness, she took walks, read books, fed the birds, attended Quaker meeting, and meditated several times a day. As fall turned to winter, she experienced an immense, spacious silence, an "interior solitude." She began to sing certain hymns over and over, like prayers. "Silently now I wait for thee. . . . Ready my God thy will to see." She knew her concept of God was intellectual and that she was being led deeper into an experience of the divine Reality, but it was beyond the ability of her mind to know how to open to it. She felt some fear. Following advice given by St. John of the Cross in *Dark Night of the Soul*, she waited in the darkness of unknowing. She began to practice the Russian Orthodox Prayer of the Heart, "Lord Jesus Christ, have mercy upon me." Eventually the prayer was reduced to one word: "Mercy." Then she stopped asking for anything, but simply directed her attention to God at all times:

> *God was in my consciousness even when my attention was on a phone call or chopping onions. I was becoming empty. Silence created space and I feared that blank expanse. I could vanish in such wilderness. As I watched ice form on the pond or walked windswept beaches I felt a falling away process. . . . I was becoming empty—blank as a meadow of snow. . . . My mind became calm. In meditation I no longer experimented with energy, mantras, colors, or visualization. I sat, silent, waiting.*[228]

At Harwich Friends Meeting on Sundays she joined in worship with others who also sat in silence and waited on God. Logs crackling in the wood-burning stove and benches creaking made the only sounds. When spring came, she reviewed scenes from her life, again giving and receiving forgiveness from people with whom she had struggled. Afterward, she felt "a bud of joy unfolding" inside; it made her sing and dance, alone at home. In silence, she opened to divine Love:

> At dawn the following day my heart opened petal by petal in surrender to Love. Blissful tears. Joy. I felt the pulse of unheard music—not familiar notes and scales but rhythm—pulsing . . . waves . . . a magnificent orchestra heard from a great distance—far grander, more passionate than earthly music. Table, window, birds, trees, oranges, refrigerator and I were the same loving energy. There was only God's Love vibrating, holding everything in its intended form. "Thank you, thank you," I said. "Thank you for every breath, for life, for pain, joy, tears, laughter, loss, for people, creatures, earth, sky, for all I know and all beyond, for mystery, for this Love."[229]

Lee felt deep humility and dropped to her knees, "feeling my smallness before the power of Love." She began to sing love songs to God. The experience continued to unfold over several days, leading her to rest ever more profoundly in divine Love:

> I lived Love, breathed praise, walked in worship, ate joy, adored God, cherished God, loved and was loved as never before. The doors of my heart stood open. Love flowed out, or in, or both, and at the same time my heart was Love. Fear was gone. I was totally safe. To die would have been simply to turn a page in a book. A deep well of happiness bubbled up in me. A fountain of love overflowed. I felt stretched thin as a soap bubble. Just as my belly stretched when I was pregnant, my soul was stretched by God's wonderful Love. The expansion was almost painful. I remembered that Jesus was supposed to be my guide and thought he must have been able to bear an even

155

greater amount of Love. I felt how accurate his words were when he said, "Perfect loves cast out fear." . . . In those days I lived in the yolk of the world, connected, nourished by God. Truth was a voice, an impulse, a knowing, a merging of mind and body. Beyond was within. . . . Paradoxes were resolved and doubts transcended.[230]

Lee became exquisitely sensitive to changes in her brain. The expansion of joy lasted until April, when it was time to leave the beach house. Anxiety returned as she faced the problems and uncertainties of the rest of her life. It was painful to feel herself shrinking, but she remained transformed, still dominated by love. At first she felt "so excited, so high from the Love coming to me that I wanted to share it with everyone. . . . Gradually I realized that Love had to be kneaded into daily life like yeast into flour."[231] Afterward she noticed that her relationships with family members were changed. She was more loving, less impatient and judgmental.

Abiding in God's Love and Power is an orientation in life, a choice we make again and again. Conservative Quaker Lloyd Lee Wilson discovered that becoming a Christian was not primarily an intellectual assent to certain ideas. It was a process of change in which he was given the desire and strength to do God's will. Following both the biblical teachings of Jesus and the inward guidance of Christ, Wilson became a pacifist:

The first great commandment is to love God totally. Therefore my first loyalty is to God, not to my country. Christ calls us to love our enemies, to pray for them, and to do good to them. I cannot do these things and also take up arms against them.[232]

While living in Norfolk, Virginia, Wilson provided counseling on conscientious objector status to soldiers and sailors who were troubled by their military involvement. He acknowledges that placing all one's trust in God can leave one feeling vulnerable:

But that is the nature of faith: to put ourselves at risk on behalf of what we believe to be true. Discipleship is costly. Even if my pacifist position results in apparent failure in the eyes of the world, I believe it is more Christ-like to suffer wrong than to oppose it by methods that are themselves wrong in Christ's sight. The standard for Christians is always faithfulness, not success.[233]

Wilson experiences the truth of Matthew 28:20, where Jesus says, *"Behold, I am with you always."* Abiding in the transforming presence of Christ has enabled him to move beyond the desire to participate in violence.

As was the case for early Friends, sometimes Quakers in our time have been able to abide in the awareness of God's Love and Power even in the midst of devastating experiences of great loss and physical suffering. Living in the cross opens eventually to joy. When German Quakers Eva and Carl Hermann were imprisoned by the Nazis, they faced the possibility of being sentenced to death. In need as she had never been before, Eva Hermann experienced the real power of intercessory prayer:

Intercession is something very serious and responsible. I have been aware again and again, often physically aware, that the prayers of my friends on the outside were helping me. It was like a wave of power which carried one further at the time when he was on the very brink of despair. On the day of our trial the prayers of our Friends, present and absent, were around us like a wall or a barricade. Later one of the prison officials said to me, "Considering what was at stake we were amazed at how calm you were." We were calm, but only through their help. . . . It can never be forgotten, and we shall ever remain in their debt.[234]

After a year of miserable imprisonment, Eva Hermann stopped experiencing it as punishment and began to discover the spiritual opportunity hidden within the stark, harsh conditions. Earlier in her life she had sung hymns declaring that God was all that was needed. Now that she was put to the test, she would discover if God really was enough:

> *I think we are all a little inclined today to listen more to that part of Jesus' most impressive commandment which is really only an appendix and an addition: thy neighbor as thyself. But who of us can love God with our whole heart, our whole soul and our whole mind? And yet it has been my experience that love of one's neighbor does not stand fast in the storms of life unless it is grounded in the love of God.*[235]

In the drab, cold prison, Hermann learned to rest more and more in God. By Christmas of 1944, her interior life was filled with Light:

> *For months we had no word of our families. Most of them had been bombed out, many of us no longer owned even what we wore, for that belonged to the prison. Our surroundings had unspeakably deteriorated; vermin abounded, the stove smoked but did not heat, the beds were made with damp covers, everything pertaining to Christmas was lacking. And yet I wrote then, "Perhaps I have never experienced Advent so strongly as this year . . . I often lie awake at night, and that which keeps me from sleeping is joy." . . . In my whole life I never had a happier Christmas. Free of all Christmas activity, it had become Christmas in the presence of God, and my heart sang: "My heart leapeth and cannot be sad."*[236]

Housed in a flimsy little factory expected to collapse during the next bombing, the political prisoners believed they would be killed before the Allied troops arrived, yet Hermann continued to abide in joy, no longer waiting for release:

> I was completely ready for anything that might come for each new day and its burdens. It was a life in the present which is eternity and I knew that no end of punishment, no pardon, no American could make me any more free than I was.[237]

When liberation finally came, life outside prison was astonishingly beautiful. Hermann was ravished by the sight and sound of birds, flowers, meadows, forests, and mountains. Post-war Germany was in ruins and the people around her were threatened by starvation. It was grim, but in prison Hermann had learned that there is an inner door to God's eternal love, a door through which she could enter, a love in which she could abide, no matter what the outward circumstances:

> In the face of the hard reality of our existence today, in the face of all the ashen gray grief which crouches on every street and before which our arms sink down in helplessness, there is for me, again and again, only the one comfort: to know that the entrance is there to reality which is greater than all the misery; that the sea of darkness is flooded over by the much greater sea of Light.[238]

This knowledge, Hermann writes, "is not won by human power, but . . . is a free gift of the grace of God.[239]

Reflection Questions

Abiding

What happens in your heart and mind when you remember your closeness to God?

What helps you stay centered, abiding in the divine Presence in all situations?

Has "a love greater than yourself" changed you or moved you to act?

What have you learned about abiding in God's Love?

Have you felt God's Love bonding you to others? Bringing your community into unity?

In what ways has your community experienced God's Power?

Perfection in the Seventeenth Century

Be perfect, therefore, as your heavenly Father is perfect. —Matthew 5:48

Preachers in seventeenth-century England insisted that nobody could attain perfection or be freed from sinning while still alive. The first Quakers were convinced, however, that Jesus would not require something of his disciples that was impossible, and they did not want to postpone perfect faithfulness until after death. Paradoxically, the first step toward perfection, after discovering the Light of Christ Within, was to become aware of how thoroughly one was failing to live according to God's ways and how insignificant and powerless one was apart from God. Perfection as a separate self was impossible. Perfection was only possible for those who surrendered their small selves and united with the divine Fountain of Love.

For early Friends, perfection was not about appearances, performance, or worldly standards. Christian perfection does not gratify a controlling ego but instead crucifies it. They endured the purifying rigors of the Refiner's Fire, dedicated their lives to following the will of God in all things—big and small—and consented to live in the cross. Friends experienced the inward Spirit of Christ teaching them, step by step, how to become perfectly responsive to God's will. Gradually, as a Friend surrendered to God, the individual's will became wholly united with the divine will. Then it was possible to enter into a different state of consciousness. Early Quakers often referred to this condition as returning to the state of "innocency" in which human beings were originally created before the fall. Innocent and trusting, Adam and Eve had at first perfectly heard and obeyed God's guidance and commands on a daily basis. They lived in a state of peace with all creation. Friends who submitted to the rigors of the spiritual journey were eventually brought, bit by bit, into the original state of harmony with God and creation. When pressed to serve as a captain in the army, early Quaker leader George Fox testified to army officials that he had entered such a state; he told them that he "lived in the virtue of that life and power that took away the occasion of all wars."* It was no longer possible for him to kill another person.

Human willpower is not capable of bringing people into a state of perfection, nor of maintaining it. Early Quakers believed, however, that Christ was making it possible to be restored to the original state in which humanity had been created, in the image and likeness of God, with a perfect, divine nature. Early Quaker writers made reference to 2 Peter 1:4:

> *He has granted to us his precious and very great promises, that through these you may escape from the corruption that is in the world . . . and become partakers of the divine nature.* (RSV)

London tract writer Rebecca Travers wrote of "that Power and Life in which we that believe have and do know the fulfilling of the promise, and are become partakers of the Divine Nature."[240]

George Fox once explained to a young man who had awakened to the divine Presence within that ahead lay three more stages of growth:

> *He took me by the hand, and said, 'young man, this is the word of the Lord to thee, there are three scriptures thou must witness to be fulfilled, first, thou must be turned from darkness to light;*

---

* "I told them I knew from whence all wars arose, even from the lusts, according to James's doctrine; and that I lived in the virtue of that life and power that took away the occasion of all wars. Yet they courted me to accept of their offer, and thought I did but compliment them. But I told them I was come into the covenant of peace, which was before wars and strifes were." George Fox, *The Journal of George Fox*, ed. John L. Nickalls (Philadelphia: Religious Society of Friends, 1995), 65.

next, thou must come to the knowledge of the glory of God; and then, thou must be changed from glory to glory.[*]

The three Scriptures that George Fox was probably referring to are as follows:

1) 1 Peter 2:9, which explains that God has called people out of darkness into his marvelous light. Early Friends understood that what Christians have called justification does not generally happen in a single moment. By continually turning attention to the Light, through the process of convincement they received the spiritual power to overcome sin, temptation, and conformity to unjust social norms.

2) 2 Corinthians 4:6 (KJV), which proclaims, For God, who commanded the light to shine out of darkness, hath shined in our hearts, to give the light of the knowledge of the glory of God. As one becomes reoriented toward the Light, one's inner senses open up, allowing openings and increasing awareness of the divine Glory, which now quietly begins to shine in the heart. Sanctification is the process of being made faithful and holy. The faithful individual and community have an increasing ability to know and carry out God's will and to participate in God's work in the world.

3) 2 Corinthians 3:18 (NKJV), which reads, But we all, with unveiled face, beholding as in a mirror the glory of the Lord, are being transformed into the same image from glory to glory. Like Moses, after he came down from speaking with God on the mountain, one who is oriented steadily and directly toward the divine Light increasingly begins to shine with divine Glory. The original divine nature in which humanity was created is restored in all who faithfully follow the Light. The glory of God becomes

---

* Quoted in Carole Dale Spencer, *Holiness: The Soul of Quakerism* (Colorado Springs, CO: Paternoster, 2007), 63–64.

visible through them. Growth in perfection entails a continuing transformation from one state of glory to a higher one. Faithfulness leads to prophetic power, and then one finally grows to the "fullness and stature of Christ."

The possibility of being restored to the state of perfect faithfulness in this life was frequently lifted up by early Friends in debates with their contemporaries. Fox wrote,

> *Christ saith, 'Be ye perfect even as my heavenly father is perfect,' for he who was perfect comes to make man and woman perfect again and bring them again to the state God made them in; so he is the maker up of the breach and the peace betwixt God and man. . . . I told them Christ was come freely, who hath perfected forever by one offering all them that are sanctified, and renews them up in the image of God, as man and woman were in before they fell; and makes man and woman's house as perfect again as God had made them at first.*[241]

As Friends grew in unity with God, through the work of the Light of Christ within, they became vessels through whom divine healing and transforming Love flowed toward others. Christ, the Light, lived and loved and acted freely and powerfully in such people.

Few early Quakers claimed to have journeyed completely into perfection, but many could point to those among them who they believed lived in a state of faithful unity with God, steadfastly fixed upon the rock that they called Christ. When speaking of perfection, early Friends often added that one grows into perfect obedience to God by degrees. More is asked of some than of others, and one is only called to be faithful "in one's measure." James Nayler wrote,

> *It is true, the Light is but manifest in the creatures by degrees, but the least degree is perfect in its measure, and being obeyed, will*

*lead to the perfect Day, and is perfect in its self,
and leads up to perfection all that perfectly
follow it.*[242]

Even those who learn to be completely faithful in their
measure need to be vigilant, however, for this is a
condition from which one can fall. Isaac Penington
described the process whereby one's inward spiritual
transformation leads toward the state of perfection:

> *For the soul truly turning to the light, the
> everlasting arm, the living power is felt; and the
> anchor being felt, it stays the soul in all troubles,
> storms, and tempests it meets with afterwards;
> which are many, yea, very many. . . . Belief in the
> light works patience, meekness, gentleness,
> tenderness, and long-suffering. It will bear
> anything for God, anything for men's souls' sake.
> It will wait quietly and stilly for the carrying on
> of the work of God in its own soul, and for the
> manifestation of God's love and mercy to others.
> It will bear the contradiction and reproach of
> sinners, seeking their good, even while they are
> plotting, contriving, and hatching mischief,
> laying many subtle snares. . . . Here is joy,
> unspeakable joy, joy which the world cannot see
> or touch, nor the powers of darkness come near
> to interrupt . . . and this joy is full of glory, which
> glory increaseth daily more and more, by the
> daily sight and feeling of the living virtue and
> power in Christ the light, whereby the soul is
> continually transformed, and changed more and
> more out of the corruptible into the incorruptible.
> . . . in them that turn towards it, give up to it, and
> abide in it. . . . It cleanseth out the thickness and
> darkness, and daily transformeth them into the
> image, purity, and perfection of the light.*[243]

Those who learn how to abide in God's Power and Love
become vessels through whom divine Power reaches out to

others. Traveling ministers Katharine Evans and Sarah Chevers, both wives and mothers, suffered many miserable imprisonments and other punishments. After setting sail to bring the Quaker message to Alexandria, Egypt, in 1658, they were imprisoned for three years by the Inquisition on the island of Malta. During one of their frequent interrogations by the Inquisitors, they said,

> By Faith we stand, and by the Power of God we are upholden; dost thou think it is by our own power and holiness we are kept from a vain conversation, from sin and wickedness?[244]

When their interrogator told them their statement was prideful, they explained that they had been "children of wrath once," like everybody else. However, God had "washed, cleansed and sanctified us through soul and spirit, in part, according to our measures, and we do press forward toward that which is perfect."[245]

In another piece of writing, Chevers described the process of self-emptying that leads to being filled and united with God. Not surprisingly, there is an ecstatic quality to her experience:

> The more we taste of this heavenly banquet, the much the more are we broken down into self denial, sealed down forever in the true poverty, and upright integrity of heart and soul, mind and conscience, wholly ransomed by the living word of life, to serve the living God. . . . [Then] we cannot hold our peace; the God . . . of glory doth open our mouth, and we speak to his praise, and utter his voice, and sound forth his word of life, and causeth the earth to tremble . . . my heart, soul and spirit that is wholly joined to the Lord, stream forth to you. . . . I am a partaker of living virtue.[246]

A beautiful description of experiencing a state of union with God was written by William Robinson after Boston magistrates condemned him to death in 1659. In a letter to fellow Quakers, Robinson describes how he is united with God's Love. Something divine flows through him to others, and it will continue to do so after his death. It is not an experience of elevated individuality; rather, he remains in community with others. He has become united with all:

> *The streams of my father's love run daily through me from the holy fountain of life to the seed throughout the whole creation. I am overcome with love, for it is my life and length of my days, it's my glory and my daily strength. I am swallowed up with love, in love I live, and with it I am overcome, and in it I dwell with the Holy Seed, to which the blessing of love is given from God who is love, who hath shed it abroad in my heart which daily fills me with living joy from the life from whence it comes. You children of the living God, feel me when you are waiting in it, when your hearts and minds are gathered into it, when . . . it runs from the fountain into your vessel, when it issues gently like new wine into your bosoms, when the strength and power of it you feel, when you are overcome with the strength of love (which is God), then feel me present in the fountain of love, wherein are many mansions.*[247]

Perfection in Our Time

Today it is popularly proclaimed that perfection is impossible for human beings. In our time, the word *perfection* is associated with a flawless outward appearance and impeccable social manners, or the ability to succeed in every arena in life, meeting the expectations of everyone. Perfectionism aimed at these goals is stressful and perpetuates unhappiness. It feeds the ego's desire for control and magnifies the sense of self. None of this is what early Friends meant when they held perfection as a goal of the spiritual life.

The early Quakers sought the kind of perfection that Jesus was speaking about in Matthew 5:48.[248] Although they often had an unconventional understanding of specific Bible passages, they did not question the translation. In our time, many look at the original Greek words used in the New Testament to get a better understanding of what Jesus meant when he told his disciples to become perfect. The Greek word used in Matthew 5:48 is *teleios*. Although *teleios* is often translated as *perfect,* it means something that has reached its goal or is "complete." In reference to the spiritual journey, another translation would be "mature" or "whole."

Today's Bible scholars also carefully consider the context of the sayings of Jesus. In Matthew 5, Jesus is instructing his disciples how to love. He is asking them to become like God, who *makes the sun rise on the evil and on the good.* He is telling them to love all, not just those who love them or who are their family members. *Love your enemies and pray for those who persecute you.* This is the way that Jesus is commanding his disciples to become perfect, as God is perfect.

In a similar passage in Luke's gospel, Jesus uses the Greek word *oiktirmon,* which can be translated as *merciful* or *compassionate.* He tells his disciples to love their enemies and pray for those who persecute them. *Be ye therefore merciful, as your Father also is merciful,* he commands. The context of both passages makes it clear that the disciples are being instructed to love in a universal way, as God does. This is not an element of the journey so much as a state toward which God draws everyone. The Christian perfection described by early Friends was a union with the divine Fountain of Love, a state attained after the "old man" was crucified and the person was born anew as a son or daughter of God. Becoming entirely faithful led to being united with the flow of God's Love for all.

Wholeness comes when something larger and wiser than the self has taken control, when God becomes the active force in a person's life and any goal other than loving faithfulness has fallen away. It may be impossible to know who has entered into a state of perfect faithfulness or true spiritual maturity. However, in looking for examples among Quakers in the past century, one twentieth-century Friend, Haverford College professor Thomas Kelly, comes to mind; his eloquent and evocative writing about the spiritual life has touched many people, and he is known for a powerful transformation late in his life that led to wholeness and radiance. Kelly is an example of a person whose lifelong desire to serve God was, for most of his adult life, mixed with the pursuit of a worldly, unhealthy perfection and a craving for social status and respect. Raised as a poor Iowa farm boy in an Evangelical Quaker family, Kelly trained as a missionary. During World War I, he worked with U.S. soldiers and then with German prisoners of war. He was fired, however, when he became a pacifist. After completing a seminary degree, he and his wife Lael went to Germany to work with the American Friends Service Committee, which was feeding starving children in that defeated nation. Afterward, Kelly pursued a PhD in philosophy at Hartford Theological Seminary. At his dissertation defense, in the stress of the moment, he was unable to answer questions. Hartford Seminary allowed him a second chance, however, and he earned his PhD.

Kelly was not satisfied to be hired as chairman of the philosophy department at a fine Midwestern college. Desiring an academic position at an elite East Coast institution, he moved his family four times in eleven years, going into debt to do so. Even after being hired by prestigious Haverford College, located near Philadelphia, Kelly still craved a doctorate from Harvard University. Harvard did not normally accept someone as a PhD candidate who had already received the same degree elsewhere, but they conceded to Kelly's strong persuasive abilities. He maintained a teaching job while taking courses and writing a second dissertation; his health suffered greatly. On the day in fall 1937 when he met to defend his Harvard dissertation, he had another attack of anxiety and could not answer the questions. Harvard would not allow him a second chance to take the exam, and he failed in his effort to earn a PhD from that university. Kelly was so distraught that his wife feared suicide. Months of deep despair followed.

Kelly's failure to achieve his ambition led to the death of the false self that had been driving him to seek worldly status. He began to feel the divine Presence in a new way; God was seeking to take hold of him. In "The Simplification of Life," Kelly describes how most people live divided lives, torn by competing desires and commitments. From personal experience, he wrote that

> over the margins of life comes a whisper, a faint call, a premonition of richer living that we know we are passing by. Strained by the very mad pace of our daily outer burdens, we are further strained by an inward uneasiness, because we have hints that there is a way of life vastly richer and deeper than all of this hurried existence, a life of unhurried serenity and peace and power. If only we could slip over into that Center![249]

What holds us back, he says, is that "we have not counted this Holy Thing within us to be the most precious thing in the world."[250]

Humbled by his failure and open to God in a new way, Kelly went to Germany in the summer of 1938 to give encouragement to Quakers there who were seeking how to be faithful during the rise of Nazism. He encountered a dire situation involving harsh persecution of any who challenged Nazi oppression. He saw the frightening threat the Nazis posed to the world. This shattered the rest of his self-centeredness. In a letter home to his wife, he wrote:

> In the midst of the work here this summer has come an increased sense of being laid hold on by a Power, a gentle, loving, but awful Power. And it

makes one know the reality of God at work in the world. And it takes away the old self-seeking, self-centered self, from which selfishness I have laid heavy burdens on you, dear one.[251]

Kelly began to live from the Center, with God, not just in moments but in a steady way. No longer torn by competing motivations, he found spiritual peace. He felt deep sympathy for the German people who risked their lives to fight Nazism, and he found that those with whom he experienced a spiritual kinship were not necessarily the well-educated but were those who, like himself, were deeply in love with a God they had directly encountered. At a Quaker gathering in Germany, Eva Hermann heard Kelly say, "I don't think that anything in this life could happen to me which would rob me of peace and joy."[252] She was skeptical at the time.

Kelly went home from Germany on fire with the Spirit and dismayed by complacent suburban American life. He gave talks that moved many people. In his home, he started an evening spiritual fellowship for interested Quaker college students. To them, he held up the itinerant ministry of George Fox as a model for their lives. When giving talks about life lived from the Center, he rarely used the pronoun, "I." His individual self had surrendered and been absorbed into a larger "we." In describing prayer, for example, he wrote:

There come times when prayer pours forth in volumes and originality such as we cannot create. It rolls through us like a mighty tide. . . . We pray, and yet it is not we who pray, but a Greater who prays in us. Something of our punctiform selfhood is weakened, but never lost. All we can say is, Prayer is taking place, and I am given to be in its orbit. In holy hush we bow in Eternity, and know the Divine Concern tenderly enwrapping us and all things within His persuading love. Here all human initiative has passed into acquiescence, and He works and prays and seeks His own through us, in exquisite, energizing life. Here the autonomy of the inner life becomes complete and we are joyfully prayed through, by a Seeking Life that flows through us into the world of human beings.[253]

Kelly's health was still strained from years of striving to fulfill his human ambition. When he woke on the morning of January 1941, he told his wife that it would be the happiest day of his life. He taught class that day, and he learned that Harper and Row was interested in publishing a collection of his essays. At home with his family that evening, while drying the supper dishes, he died of a heart attack. Afterward, Kelly's colleague, Douglas Steere, compiled a little book from five of Kelly's talks. Published as *A Testament of Devotion*, it became one of the most popular Christian devotional books of the twentieth century, providing a beloved guide to people across the spectrum of Christian theology.

Several years later, while Eva Hermann was in a Nazi prison and groping to find God in the barren misery of her circumstances, she began to sense that Thomas Kelly was near to her in some spiritual way: "I never had any personal contact with him. Yet, while I was in prison I felt his presence from one day to the next, stronger and stronger. . . . And I let him take my hand and lead me."[254] After the war, Friends sent Hermann a copy of *Testament of Devotion*. She found it described much that she had experienced in prison,

expressed more clearly and understandably and beautifully than I can ever say it. . . . It is like a map which urges me on to ever new discoveries in a country into which I ventured under his leadership, and there took a few first hesitating steps. To penetrate it further, to come to feel at home there, seems to me to be the sole worthwhile fulfillment of life.[255]

Marjorie Sykes is another twentieth-century Friend who was a model for many of growth toward Christian perfection. Born in England and educated at Oxford, she went to India to be a teacher soon after receiving her university degree, later serving as principal of a school for girls. After the world-renowned poet Rabindranath Tagore invited her to serve on the staff of his innovative school, she nurtured the worship experiences of Christian students and engaged in interfaith dialogue. After Tagore's death, Sykes became a teacher at the Women's Christian College in Chennai, India, insisting upon living in an impoverished neighborhood nearby rather than on the school campus. She drew her own water at the local well in the morning, cooked her meals over a wood stove, and rode her bicycle to work. Sykes also supported a village orphanage and adopted a teenage girl who wanted an education. By the time India gained independence in 1947, she had already lived almost half her life in that country. She became an Indian citizen.

Mahatmas Gandhi invited Sykes to live at his ashram. After his death, she trained teachers for the "new education" Gandhi had designed. Students worked first in community to acquire and demonstrate real-world skills in growing food, spinning cloth, cooking, sanitation, carpentry, and maintenance before being trained as teachers. In 1957 Sykes helped to bring alive another of Gandhi's ideas by convening a "Peace Army" of women trained to peacefully address situations of conflict in their home communities. In the summer of 1964 she was invited to the United States and Canada to help train people for work in the Civil Rights Movement.

On one occasion Sykes was called upon to give a public talk at Quaker House in New Delhi to replace a speaker who was ill. Martha Dart, her biographer, wrote that while Sykes spoke, "A Power was transmitted through the words, and many present were moved to tears."[256] Sykes also sensed that Power. She responded in a letter to Dart:

What you say . . . confirms my own feeling that some of the time I was mysteriously being

173

*"spoken through," as happens in a meeting for
Worship that is "in the Life". . . . I did have notes
but there was something that took over the
shaping of the talk regardless of the notes. And I
am deeply grateful that this was channeled to
your needs. But I still feel it is somehow out of
place to "thank" the one who at such times
becomes the channel—we need together to thank
that Great Life in which we have moved.*[257]

A strict vegetarian, Sykes grew much of her own food.
After leaving Gandhi's ashram, she lived in a very simple
house on the side of a steep mountain, with no running
water and no electricity. Visitors noted the simplicity,
order, and discipline of her life, as well as the peace they
felt in her home. Several felt that something of her order
and discipline was imparted to them during their visits,
leaving them feeling at though they had somehow been
inwardly cleansed.[258] Another visitor was affected by the
spiritual power she encountered in Sykes:

*I am more and more impressed with the spiritual
force that emanates from Marjorie. There is
something about her—some rare quality which is
very hard to put into words. It was a real
adventure of the spirit to visit her. She is a
forceful, dynamic, gifted person—so perceptive of
little things about you that you wonder if she is
reading your mind.*[259]

In 1974 Sykes gave talks and classes in Asia, the United
States, the Pacific Islands, New Zealand, and Australia. She
spoke of nonviolence, simplicity, and self-discipline; she
also discussed which forms of aid and trade were harmful.
In the United States she commented upon the "overfed
atmosphere" she found there. Her critique was accepted,
and people were deeply affected by her presence. One
person said, "I don't really remember what she said
because what she was—the spirit that emanated from her—
was so powerful, it took precedence over everything

else."[260] Another wrote that Sykes's lifestyle was an inspiration to many, providing a model for addressing environmental problems by living sustainably. There was a sense of a divine Presence moving through Sykes, "Her classes were on fire. She was a real channel for the Spirit to speak through and something out beyond her often took over and worked through her."[261]

Sykes never married but was bonded in friendship to two fellow British Friends, Alice Barnes and Mary Barr, who had also spent much of their adult lives in India as teachers and educators. For many years after retirement, they lived near each other in simple cottages in rural Kotagiri, in the Nilgiri Hills. Called the "Quaker Trio" by locals, they met together weekly for meeting for worship, sometimes joined by a visitor. Barnes wrote about how different they were from each other, yet their meetings for worship were often gathered, "and when looking into one another's eyes at the end, we have known beyond any manner of doubt, and with no need for words, that we have been together in the Holy of Holies."[262]

At 81, Sykes was living in Rasulia Friends Centre, a Quaker center in India. She insisted on cooking meals for guests who visited her there, and she was still sewing her own clothes. During the final years of her life, she lived in a retirement home in England. When Linda Hibbs came to visit, Sykes was 89 and working on the manuscript for her book *Indian Tapestry*. She left a vivid impression on her visitor, who remembers, above all, Sykes's "radiant smile." Hibbs came away with a sense of her "laser-like intensity of purpose and her constant cleaving to careful truth."[263] Sykes's biographer, Martha Dart, felt that the most significant aspect of Marjorie Sykes was not her extraordinary experiences and actions, nor her "penetrating and challenging" words, but, "the force of Spirit that comes through her."[264]

Today, as in the past, Friends point to humility as a sign of someone's closeness to God. A truly humble person would likely disagree that they have entered a state anything like perfect faithfulness to God's will or union with God's Love. In their humility, they see their flaws more clearly than others. When I talked with Friends about the contemporary Quaker experience of perfection, many people spoke about Bill Taber, a quiet Conservative Friend known for his wisdom, compassion, and humility. Earlham College professor of religion Michael Birkel wrote,

As a teacher, writer, speaker, retreat leader, and spiritual nurturer, Bill Taber touched the lives of many, including Quakers of all theological sorts. Many Friends who had been wounded by their experience of an exclusive Christianity found themselves healed by Bill's generous understanding of the gospel. Bill was deeply gifted in worship, not only in vocal ministry and prayer, but also in a radiant silence that drew others into a greater sense of the Divine Presence. His gentle, centered spirit invited all around him to turn inward and encounter God afresh.[265]

I remember times when I sat near Bill Taber in meeting for worship and felt strengthened by doing so. Once, when encountering him walking on an outdoor path, his gentle smile conferred a blessing. Many people sought him out for spiritual counsel, and he was an excellent teacher of the Quaker spiritual life, taking his students into the experience of the things he was teaching about.

In the hours and days after Taber's death in 2005, several Friends who had felt a call to Quaker ministry had a sense of his presence, giving them encouragement to follow the call. Ten years after his passing, people still speak reverently about how their experience of his teaching, guidance, or simple presence has been an ongoing source of light and healing in their lives. At Quaker gatherings in places where he lived, worked, and worshipped, those who knew him— and some who did not—sometimes sense his presence. Like this Friend, many who have grown most fully into a life of faithful union with God would appear simple and humble, outwardly unremarkable to others.

Reflection Questions

Perfection

When have you felt God's Love flowing through you?

Have you known someone whose life modeled faithfulness in matters big and small? Have you met a person who seemed to radiate divine Love, Peace, or Power?

Has your spiritual experience given confidence in the power of God to transform your mind and heart and restore the divine image within you? In others?

Do you aspire to live with God in a measure of love, truth, and obedience that could be complete? Why or why not?

The Spiritual Journey

Do you sense that there is an underlying spiritual journey common to all Quakers, all Christians, and/or all seekers?

How do the ten elements of the spiritual journey described in this book help you understand or explore the nature of your own experience?

What light does this book shed on the common spiritual journey of your faith community?

One Friend's Spiritual Journey

People experience the spiritual journey differently. The ten strands of the journey that I have named in this book appear in many varied ways. They are all interconnected and blend into one another. I offer brief descriptions of my own experiences as a way to reveal how these strands can weave through a particular person's life. I hope that readers will be moved to explore with one another their own experiences of these elements of the spiritual journey.

Longing

Raised as a Christian, I grew up loving Jesus. At age twelve, I attended a friend's week-long Bible camp. Every evening we gathered for a service under the pine trees. On the first night, in response to much encouragement, I went up to the altar to invite Jesus into my heart. I was given a Bible and a little blue book into which I could write that momentous date. Later, however, when I returned home and reflected about this, I sensed that Jesus had always been inside me, long before attending that camp. This understanding satisfied me for a while.

As I grew, I had glimpses of the sacred mystery at the heart of life. When I lay in my tree-filled back yard looking up into the sky, I sensed the vastness of the cosmos and felt small. Sometimes I read books about spiritual matters. In my late twenties, my interest in spiritual matters turned into a deep longing. My grandfather died in a sudden accident, and a man I loved had a life-threatening illness. My heart ached. My studies at graduate school began to feel like a dead end; they were not leading me to real meaning. Finally, nothing was more important than understanding what life was really about and what would happen after death. I took walks alone at night under the stars. I yearned for something I couldn't name. I longed to know God directly—if God, indeed, existed. I took out the

Bible I'd been given in Bible camp long ago. An index card fell out. In my sixth-grade handwriting, I had copied these words: *Then you will call upon me and come and pray to me, and I will hear you. You will seek me and find me; when you seek me with all your heart* (Jeremiah 29:12–13 RSV). I was moved by God's promise to find those who seek God with all their heart.

Seeking

I was still in elementary school when I began seeking to understand life and know God. I questioned my Sunday School teachers. Under night skies glittering with stars, the mysterious nature of existence seemed more clear than in the daytime. During my freshman year of college, I began to doubt the existence of God and stopped attending church services. However, three years later, when my heart was broken at the end of my first serious romance, I began to seek to understand the nature of reality. Did God exist? Within a few years, this search became more important than anything else. I went to the library and took out all the books I could find about religion and spiritual experience. My housemate, who had studied meditation with Buddhist monks, brought home the latest books about spirituality from the bookstore where she worked. We read them and speculated together about spiritual matters. Then we found a teacher of meditation and engaged in spiritual practices for hours every day. I attended lectures, listened to tapes, and took classes. Later I began to read the Bible daily, along with books about other religions.

After moving to Philadelphia, I visited local churches, looking for a spiritual home. Then, on my thirty-fourth birthday, I attended a workshop at Pendle Hill, a Quaker retreat and study center. I was deeply moved by my experience there and knew I had found my community. I started attending the nearest Quaker meeting, and I set about learning all I could about Quaker faith and practice.

After becoming a Quaker, at times I continued to seek larger spiritual openness by practicing meditation with Buddhists, Hindus, Jews, and Sufis. More than once I participated in a Native American-style sweat lodge. Even now, after two decades of deepening immersion in direct experience and the Quaker spiritual life, I continue at times to attend lectures and workshops, take classes, read books, and seek people who might broaden my understanding.

Turning Within

Transcendental Meditation (TM) came to the United States when I was in high school. I spent my babysitting money to take the course and for several months practiced meditation every morning. However, I could not sustain a daily practice. A course in the French existentialists during college introduced me to the idea that there might be no purpose to life apart from whatever meaning we create for ourselves. Several of my professors implied that there is no God, no consciousness or intelligence beyond humanity, and many friends, including my boyfriend, believed the same. Doubting the existence of a Supreme Being, I stopped attending church services.

I imagined that was the end of my spiritual life, but I discovered that in many respects it was the beginning. Now I had to find out for myself the nature of existence and discover a just way to live in a world filled with poverty and hunger. Without the church's guidelines regarding sexuality, I had to decide for myself the right way to be in relationship with my boyfriend. My questions about life became even more compelling at the end of my first romance three years later. I walked in the woods and looked up at the night sky, wondering where God was.

When someone I loved had a fatal illness, I felt it was important to discover what happens after death. Is our consciousness annihilated, or does it continue beyond our physical form? By then I had lost hope of discovering the answers in books or through attending lectures. Needing to know directly for myself, I finally began to seek the answers within. In the daytime, I walked to the fields on the edge of town. At night, under dark, starry skies, I walked the hilly streets of Amherst, Massachusetts. I wrote in my journal, uncovering painful emotions, and paid attention to my dreams. I waited for understanding, for direct insight, for a sign that God was real. I was praying with all my heart.

Now, decades later, turning within is something I must remember to do many times a day, each time I notice that my thoughts and actions have become fragmented or anxious. I have learned many methods that help me to pay inward attention: deep breathing, letting go of what I'm trying to control, praying, meditation, calling on Jesus, sensing my connection to the earth, turning to the still, sacred place within, offering my concerns up to God.

Openings

In my late twenties, during my time of wholehearted seeking and turning within, my perception opened. One night while walking under a night sky, by grace, I glimpsed what George Fox called "the hidden Unity in the Eternal Being." From deep within me, I suddenly knew that the stars and I are part of a vast oneness. A divine Light flows through us and through all things. I felt this Light flowing through me, down my arms, and out my fingertips into the world. I knew that the power of this divine Light is so great that it can heal any problem on earth, no matter how terrible. I was changed forever by this glimpse of the invisible, divine Reality that undergirds everything and of which I am a part. It took time before I could use the word God for the oneness and the Light I had experienced, but from that moment forward, I no longer doubted that I am part of an eternal spiritual reality.

I started devoting time every day to learning and practicing ways to pray and meditate. The more I paid attention inwardly, the more was revealed to me. Day by day I was shown how God was—and had been—at work in all the affairs of my life. I saw more clearly the relationship between my inner life and outer experience. Through prayer, images, dreams, and silent waiting, I received guidance in matters small and large.

In the decades that followed, there have been some dry spells in my life, periods when openings are infrequent. Nonetheless, over time I continue to be given glimpses and reminders of divine Truth and Love. Step by step, sometimes quickly and sometimes slowly, I am shown the path that God would have me walk.

Refiner's Fire

Since early childhood I have frequently felt embarrassed by my social awkwardness or experienced pain because of various failures. As I learned to pay attention inwardly and know the presence of God within, I gradually came to see a difference between judging myself by social norms and being shaped by something deeper. Embarrassment and shyness are different from the uncomfortable sensations that come when I act without love or integrity. I have learned to see more quickly when my words or actions spring from fear, hurt, or a desire to control and to become aware when my behavior causes harm or impedes a group process. If I keep paying attention, sometimes I am shown that I need to apologize or make amends. This is humbling. When I obey, however, healing happens in my relationships, within me, and possibly within others as well.

Sometimes I have felt pain after giving vocal ministry that was not entirely faithful. More than once, I softened the sharp point of a message by wrapping it in a story or in ideas. Once, when someone complimented me on such a message, I felt an acute sense of how I had been unfaithful. I receive ongoing lessons in how to speak simply and clearly as prompted by the Spirit, without preface, embellishment, or neat conclusions. As I learn from my mistakes and take time to seek the truth, my ability to discern the promptings of the Spirit from other motivations slowly becomes sharper.

Images, memories, dreams, and inner words or phrases come to show me when something is out of kilter in what I'm thinking or doing or in the direction toward which I'm headed. The Refiner's Fire is an apt metaphor for experiences when the Light has revealed what is out of God's order in myself and/or my participation in my culture. On a couple of occasions when I've been bent on going in a certain direction and didn't want to see it wasn't God's path for me, I've been woken up night after night with inner heat and brightness showing me what is not right until I accept the truth of what I'm being shown. Sometimes this has led me to make large and difficult changes in my life and to give up opportunities I wanted to pursue.

In the light of the Refiner's Fire, I am becoming less controlled by fear and the desire for comfort and status and more able to live from my connection to God's Love and Truth. At times, I am aware of a very slow, subtle process of inward purification, simplification, and healing that is taking place, freeing me of mental, emotional, and spiritual bondage that I was often not aware of until it fell away. Sometimes I have had glimpses of the mostly hidden work of Christ freeing and healing me.

Community

During my childhood, my family engaged in meals, chores, church, travel, and fun together in a way that established a firm foundation in life. When I went to college, however, I stopped living with my family and soon thereafter left the church of my childhood. As a young woman, I did not have a community sufficient to support the person I was becoming. During the years of spiritual seeking that followed, I journeyed with a few companions for periods of time. For several years I studied with a teacher, an outward spiritual guide, but much of the time I was alone with my big questions and the inward Guide.

When I began to attend Quaker meeting on Sunday mornings, I dreamed I had been swimming laps alone in a big pool, developing strength, and now I was joining a team. Henceforth my spiritual journey would not be a solitary one. At meeting I was drawn together with people of all ages, folks with unique personalities, gifts, and quirks. We engaged in worship, study, discussion, potluck meals, small groups, and committee meetings. I formed friendships with many older people. Most formative was participating in the business meeting. Time and again, as the members and attenders of my Quaker meeting struggled to collectively discern God's will for our decisions, we were joined into a corporate body. In my meeting and in larger groups of Friends, I gave and received help, guidance, understanding, challenge, and love. I was no longer an individual floating through life but an integral part of a community.

After twenty-two years living among Quakers in the Philadelphia area, I spent three years in the small midwestern city of Richmond, Indiana. I attended two of the three Quaker meetings in Richmond and discovered I already knew some of the Friends in town because I had met them at Quaker gatherings. Both those I knew and those I didn't extended the hand of friendship to me. I joined with them in worship, committee meetings, business meetings, potlucks, small groups, fellowship, and conversations. I soon discovered how these two Quaker meetings were seeking to discern and follow their collective call into faithfulness. I felt how all of us were part of a larger, worldwide Quaker body, as well as an even larger body of people all over the world seeking to know God and bring God's Love more fully into the world.

Leadings

Long before I had any idea that my life was being guided toward God's purposes, I sometimes sensed and followed divine leadings. Intuitive guidance whose nature I did not understand prompted me to choose one man rather than another as my first serious boyfriend, and this guidance also sent me back home to the United States each time I traveled to Europe and wanted to settle there. These inward promptings were connected to a sense of a mysterious destiny or purpose for my life, which I did not examine at the time. Only many years later did I begin to understand that I, like others, had been born to participate in God's healing purposes for humanity and the earth.

About a year after I started attending a Quaker meeting, I questioned whether I had joined the right community. My intense spiritual experiences seemed too "far out" for some Friends. However, many inner and outer events showed me that I was, indeed, where God wanted me to be. A particularly vivid dream showed me that the Religious Society of Friends has a very important role to play in God's plan of healing for the world and that in order to faithfully play that role, spiritual renewal among Friends is needed. My call involves helping Quakers, especially liberal Friends, develop a more open-hearted faith in God in order that we may make our true contribution to the world. I am one of many people who have been called in that way.

In 1995 I received a leading to write an article for *Friends Journal* about the direct spiritual experiences of both early and contemporary Friends. Writing that article opened doors. I was invited to be a co-facilitator of a 1996 Pendle Hill workshop on mysticism among Friends today. Out of that, other opportunities appeared, and more leadings. I have been led, step by step, to write articles, pamphlets, a blog, and now this book. I was also led to be a teacher of courses and workshops, usually for small honoraria, if anything.

Then, for four years, I served as resident Quaker studies teacher at Pendle Hill. I participated in joint leadings with other Friends, including organizing many intergenerational Quaker women's gatherings; fifteen years of tri-annual gatherings to help deepen the spiritual experience of

Friends; and a prayer vigil for peace at the Liberty Bell that continued every Sunday afternoon for many years. I have been led to study and share about the spiritual experiences of Friends at the beginning of Quakerism in order to help Friends today renew our openness to the direct inspiration of God and Christ.

I have also experienced God's leadings in relation to many personal details of my life and living arrangements. For two and a half years I lived in the inner city of Philadelphia as a member of a "ministry of presence" there, working with neighbors to reclaim a park from drug dealers and make a safer place for children to play.

More recently, in my fifties, I have followed a leading to marriage. Terry Hauger and I had both been single for many decades of our adult lives. Our discernment process lasted years, during which we were both learning to know ourselves better as well as learning to love another person in new ways. We had to discern among our own desires and fears and the true leading of the Spirit. It took a long time to clearly hear God's still, small voice of love calling us to marriage. Our relationship is also an ongoing opportunity to learn how, as a couple, we can share this love with family, community, and others.

The Cross

Learning to live in accordance with God's intentions for my life involves an ongoing struggle with my desire to stay with what is familiar, easy, and comfortable. I am faced with "the cross to my own will" many times every day. Sometimes living in the cross means putting aside my own needs and preoccupations to give full attention and service to another person; at other times it means I must say "not now" to others in order to attend to something to which God is calling me. In writing this book, it has often meant staying home revising another chapter instead of going to various interesting events. At times, it has meant waiting for God's leading to become clear even when I am eager to take action; at other times, it means acting even when I would prefer to spend more time in preparation. When anxious, it means sitting with my discomfort and turning it over to God in prayer instead of giving in to strong temptations to block out my feelings with distractions. Even in caring for my body I'm asked to surrender to God's will by abstaining from tasty junk food or products whose production harms the earth.

To follow my call, I have given up much that constitutes a middle-class life in my country. Until the age of fifty-five, I remained single and never owned a house or car. I did not have children. With the exception of the four years I worked full-time at Pendle Hill, I took only part-time or temporary jobs. For most of my adult life, I lived without health insurance. Usually I had little money in the bank and relatively few material possessions, apart from book-cases full of mostly second-hand books. Often I lived in the homes of others. For housing and transportation, as well as for spiritual and financial support, I was dependent on others in a way that was humbling and uncomfortable. An awesome number of wonderful people have offered support of many kinds. Although I have felt vulnerable, this way of living allowed me to be open and available to people in ways I would not have been if I had been focusing on earning enough income to pay for a home of my own. These choices involved sacrifice, but they also freed me to do the learning, teaching, spiritual nurture, organizing, and writing to which I felt God leading me.

I first understood the significance of the cross in my life when I was excluded from a wonderful opportunity after asking questions, speaking uncomfortable truths, and insisting on discernment. I felt I had been faithful, if imperfectly, so I had difficulty understanding why my concerns were dismissed and I was rejected. Pain and confusion about this persisted for a long time. Then one evening, while staying at a Franciscan retreat center and praying in a room near a large, colorful image of the crucifixion, I asked for understanding. In my prayer, a startling response came back. "Come join me on the cross," Jesus seemed to say.

After some initial resistance, I imagined doing so. I felt Jesus welcoming my companionship on the cross. I sensed his love, compassion, and understanding. A sweet consolation filled me, wiping away my pain. I remembered that being faithful does not necessarily lead to worldly success. Speaking truth and asking hard questions does not always meet with approval.

Abiding

In carrying out a difficult leading to create a new program, I and the members of a team I was working with felt sustained by God. At the lowest points in life, as well, when my energy levels have been low or my health poor, when I have felt incapable of acting, I have felt God's great Love and Power working through me. During periods when I have experienced humbling rejections, failures, or criticism, when I am tempted to despair, I have been learning to turn my attention to God's goodness and away from the storms of my ego and emotions. I am remembering to rest in God more quickly when I find myself in confusion or distress.

Since the time I first dedicated my life to God's purposes, I have been asked again and again to face my fears and go beyond them. When I feel God asking me to take steps that seem risky or difficult, I tend to resist, hesitate, and look around for material reassurance or someone else to take on the task. Sometimes I stay stuck in this for a long time. Eventually, however, grace helps me to trust and be faithful. When I trust, I feel God's Love for me, for others, for this world. Then, I am at peace. Sometimes I feel spiritual power move through me when I speak or write. Sometimes I don't feel any power but witness external changes or the arrival of surprisingly hopeful possibilities and gracious assistance, what Quakers call "way opening." Tasks or situations that had previously seemed too difficult or impossible then seem possible, even inviting.

Perfection

I have experienced perfection only in brief glimpses—previews, perhaps, of a future state that beckons to me. There have been some moments when I feel perfectly in harmony with God's desires for me, in the flow of life, walking in the Light, empowered by grace to do whatever I am called to do, whether that be a small task or a larger one. Once in a while I am able to sense how God has been working within to free me and make me more receptive to divine Love, better able to pass on love and truth and peace to others.

I still have many internal impediments to perfect union with God, but I feel called to continue on the path toward divine Love. When I was in my late twenties, I had a powerful dream (or vision) in which I experienced the completion for which I was born. I was standing on a bare floor when I sensed that God was asking me to let go of "holding myself up." In the dream, I felt at first a great deal of resistance, afraid that I would smack painfully on the floor if I let go. Then, as I remembered ways that God had sustained me in the past, I began to trust in God's ability to sustain me even if I let go. In trust, I let myself fall backward, and my heart slowly opened. As it opened, I began to dissolve into a loving divine Light. This Love was so beautiful that my heart opened more and more fully to it. Before I could hit the floor, I had completely opened up into this loving golden Light. I became one with God's Love. Nothing else existed.

I believe this was a dream not only of my life's goal but a vision of what is possible for all of us.

The Spiritual Journey in Our Time

During the years I was reading accounts of early Friends and writing this book, many people asked me what is the value of studying the past when there is so much urgency in the present. Indeed, humanity faces great challenges. Environmental destruction and worldwide economic instability could bring disasters of great magnitude. In order to survive the social and ecological changes that have been set in motion by our disruption of the planet's ecology, the human race needs to respond with a shift of consciousness sufficient to dramatically change our collective behavior. We need to learn to live with one another, and with all of creation, in healing and sustainable ways.

Important changes were ushered into the world through the faithful efforts of many Quakers described in these pages. Their struggles, experiments, and discoveries helped to make space for something new in human thinking and being. Seventeenth-century Quakers contributed significantly to new experiments in religious freedom, democracy, and equality. Contemporary Friends have continued to bring greater truth and love into individual lives and communities and also into global and national systems. Many of the courageous Friends whose stories are told in these pages responded to God as fully and purely as they could. They modeled human behavior and relationships based on the sacred nature of people and creation. As they did so, the divine impulse was freed to act through them in transforming ways. Their experience of the direct nature of the human connection to God has much to teach us all.

Only with divine guidance and only by allowing divine wisdom and healing to come through us can we collectively make the shift of consciousness needed in our time. It is crucial, therefore, to wake up more fully to our relationship to the indwelling Spirit of God and to our place in creation. To follow the divine will for us in this time of change, it will not be sufficient to believe that Christ—or any other sacred being—has already saved us. Something more fundamental than just this *belief* is required. We must fully wake up to the divine Reality that suffuses the world and makes all things sacred. We, too, must grow into our inheritance as sons and daughters of God.

Recognizing God's Presence within and among us, we can be guided by the Light in everything we do. The Eternal Being is knocking upon the heart of each person, waiting to be acknowledged and welcomed into our awareness, wanting to create, through us, heaven on earth. Both as individuals and as communities, we must learn to welcome the Spirit to live and move and act through us. We must become as bold as the early Quakers who found Christ within them and allowed Christ to act through them. Only God can do what is needed in our time, and God will only do it through a willing humanity aware of its interconnections with other people, the planet, and all that is holy.

The experiences of the passionate seventeenth-century and contemporary people in these pages can teach us a great deal about what is required of us now. I pray that we will sense more keenly the transformation that God wants to bring about in our time and learn how we can fully and joyfully dedicate ourselves to participating in the creation of an evolved humanity and a renewed world. Then, as fully realized children of God, we can let go of the past and enter something entirely new.

All who are led by the Spirit of God are sons of God. For you did not receive the spirit of slavery to fall back into fear, but you have received the spirit of sonship. When we cry, "Abba! Father!" it is the Spirit himself bearing witness with our spirit that we are children of God, and if children, then heirs, heirs of God and fellow heirs with Christ, provided we suffer with him in order that we may also be glorified with him. I consider that the sufferings of this time are not worth comparing with the glory that is to be revealed to us. For the creation waits with eager longing for the revealing of the sons of God . . . because the creation itself will be set free from its bondage to decay and obtain the glorious liberty of the Children of God. (Romans 8:14–19, 21 RSV)

ACKNOWLEDGMENTS

This is a small book, but creating it
has been a large undertaking, supported by many.
I am immensely grateful for so much help over the years during
my search to understand and write about the journey described
in these pages. I'm thankful to so many more people and
institutions than I can name. May God bless you all as
bountifully as you have blessed me!

To my husband, Terry Hauger, for steadfast companionship,
love, and support.

To my parents, Jean and Charlie Martin,
for life and love, and for raising me up with so much goodness.
To Laurie, Cindy, Chris, Kate, Robert, Barry, Fred, Alex, Leila,
and Miles, for being such a wonderful family.

To the elders, teachers, and spiritual companions who helped me
learn about the spiritual journey, including Bill Taber, Sonnie
Cronk, Ken and Katharine Jacobsen, Chris Ravendal,
Barbarajene Williams, Susan Smith, Diane Bonner, Dorothy
Reichardt, Richard Siebels, Louise Mullen, Connie Lezenby,
Anne Pomeroy, Elaine Emily, Alison Levie, Michael Wajda, Tony
Prete, Ted Perry, Maia Tapp, Lauri Perman, and Michael Birkel.

To all who provided holy accompaniment and helped with
discernment in following my call, including the members of three
committees who've had care and oversight of this ministry,
especially Amey Hutchins, Mickey Abraham, Nell Kahil, and
Kody Hersh, and the members of my four peer groups, as well as
the Evergreens. To my Anchorette sisters, Laura Melly, Martha
Kemper, Viv Hawkins, Hollister Knowlton, and Carolyn Schodt.

To Chestnut Hill and Newtown Square Meetings
for recognizing and supporting my call to ministry.
To all the many people who have offered encouragement, prayer,

love, feedback, accompaniment, food, housing, rides, practical support, and financial assistance. Especially big thanks to those who shared their homes with me for extended periods: Hollister Knowlton, Jorge Araúz, Laura Melly, Jackie Speicher, Scott and Susan Rhodewalt, Ruth and Sam Neff, Jeanne Dubino and Steve Tuck. Gratitude to Carolyn Schodt, Mike Resman, Elizabeth Gordon, Kaki Sjogren, and Barb Smith whose particularly generous gifts made it possible to start and finish this book.

To the many Friends who shared their spiritual experiences with me, both privately and for this book. To the people and publishers who graciously granted permission to include their words. To Swarthmore, Earlham, and Haverford Colleges for their Friends Historical and Quaker Collections.

To Carole Spencer, Brian Drayton, Cynthia Bourgeault, Amy Lyles Wilson, Paul Buckley, Helene Pollock, Paul Rasor, Rene Lape, Beth Lawn, Terry Hauger, Kathy McKay, and others who reviewed this manuscript at various stages. The remaining errors are mine! To Charles Martin of Inner Light Books, to whom I am deeply grateful for editing and publishing this book.

To Friends Center, Pendle Hill retreat center, Friends General Conference, *What Canst Thou Say?*, Ben Lomond Quaker Center, Powell House, Chestnut Hill Meeting, West Richmond Friends Meeting, Clear Creek Meeting, Milwaukee Meeting, Ithaca Meeting, and Beloit Meeting for opportunities to share and discuss this material.

To the Lyman Fund, for a grant in 1996.
To the Clarence and Lilly Pickett Endowment, for a grant for Quaker leadership in 2001.
To Pendle Hill for the Kenneth L. Carroll Scholarship, for two terms in residence in 2005.
To Earlham School of Religion and the Mullen family, for the Mullen Writing Fellowship in 2013.

To early Friends and other inspired prophets, mystics, visionaries, and fools for God who made the journey, gave over their small selves for divine purposes, and told their stories.

Grateful acknowledgment is made for permission to quote from copyrighted material (continued from the copyright page):

To *Friends Journal* (www.friendsjournal.org) to quote from "God Can Speak to Each of Us" by Hayo Daniella © 2005 Friends Publishing Corporation; "Africa, Appalachia, and Arrest" by Eileen Flanagan © 2013 Friends Publishing Corporation; "A Clerk's Lesson From Occupy" by Robert Hernblad © 2013 Friends Publishing Corporation; "A Quaker Life in India: Marjorie Sykes" by Linda Hibbs © 1998 Friends Publishing Corporation; "Send Me" by Deborah Saunders © 1998 Friends Publishing Corporation; "Strained, Breathless, and Hurried: Learning from the Life of Thomas R. Kelly" by Chad Thralls © 2011 Friends Publishing Corporation; "How Quakers Make Decisions (It's Not Just Consensus!)" (video) edited by Jon Watts © 2014; and "A Statement of Christian Pacifism" by Lloyd Lee Wilson © 2003 Friends Publishing Corporation.

To Pendle Hill Publications for permission to quote from several books and pamphlets, as listed in the bibliography and notes.

To Timothy Ashworth, Micah Bales, Elizabeth Ann Blackshine, Stephanie Crumley-Effinger, Ben Pink Dandelion, Steven Davison, Paula Deming, Jessica Easter, Elaine Emily, Jennifer Elam, Chuck Fager, Charlotte Fardelmann, John Fitch, Eileen Flanagan, Thomas Gates, Lola Georg, Michael Gibson, Eden Grace, Elizabeth Gordon, Gerald Hewitson, Amy Kietzman, Linda Caldwell Lee, Noah Baker Merrill, Peggy Senger Morrison, Parker Palmer, Rhonda Pfaltzgraff-Carlson, Helene Pollock, Michael Resman, Arthur O. Roberts, Bill Samuel, Deborah Saunders, Steve Smith, Robert K. Taylor, Cathy Walling, Jon Watts, Alex Wildwood, and Lloyd Lee Wilson.

Notes

[1] For example, William Dewsbury, quoted in Joseph A. Besse, *A Collection of the Sufferings of the People Called Quakers . . .* (London: L. Hinde, 1753), 2:525; George Fox, *The Journal of George Fox,* ed. John

[2] Sarah Blackborow, *A Visit to the Spirit in Prison . . .* (London: Printed for Thomas Simmons, 1658), 9.

[3] Blackborow, *A Visit to the Spirit,* 7.

[4] Mary Penington, "Some Account of Circumstances in the Life of Mary Penington, 1821," in *Hidden in Plain Sight: Quaker Women's Writings 1650–1700,* ed. Mary Garman et al. (Wallingford, PA: Pendle Hill Publications, 1996), 220.

[5] Margaret Fell, "A Relation of Margaret Fell, Her Birth, Life, Testimony, and Sufferings," in *Hidden in Plain Sight: Quaker Women's Writings 1650–1700,* ed. Mary Garman et al. (Wallingford, PA: Pendle Hill Publications, 1996), 245.

[6] Stephen Crisp, "Journal of the Life of Stephen Crisp," in *Early Quaker Writings, 1650–1700,* ed. Hugh Barbour and Arthur O. Roberts (Wallingford, PA: Pendle Hill Publications, 2004), 199.

[7] Joan Vokins, "God's Mighty Power Magnified," in *Hidden in Plain Sight: Quaker Women's Writings 1650–1700,* ed. Mary Garman et al. (Wallingford, PA: Pendle Hill Publications, 1996), 256.

[8] Quoted in Marcelle Martin, "Awakening Today," *A Whole Heart* (blog), January 22, 2013, para. 5, accessed December 9, 2015, http://awholeheart.com/ 2013/01/22/.

[9] Quoted in Martin, "Awakening Today," para. 4.

[10] Margaret Hope Bacon, *Love Is the Hardest Lesson: A Memoir* (Wallingford, PA: Pendle Hill Publications, 1999), 22.

[11] Steve Smith, *A Quaker in the Zendo,* Pendle Hill Pamphlet #370 (Wallingford, PA: Pendle Hill Publications, 2004), 5.

[12] Steve Smith, *A Quaker in the Zendo,* Pendle Hill Pamphlet #370 (Wallingford, PA: Pendle Hill Publications, 2004), 4.

[13] Quoted in Martin, "Awakening Today," para. 3.

[14] Jessica Easter, personal email to author, July 7, 2014.

15 Quoted in Edward Smith, *William Dewsbury c1621–1688: One of the first Valiant Sixty Quakers* (York, England: Sessions Book Trust, 1997; facsimile of 1836 book, London: Darton and Harvey), 25.

16 Quoted in Rosemary Moore, *The Light in Their Consciences: Early Quakers in Britain; 1646–1666* (University Park: Pennsylvania State University Press, 2000), 37.

17 Quoted in Emily Manners, *Elizabeth Hooton: The First Quaker Woman Preacher (1600–1672)* (London: Headley Brothers, 1914), 4.

18 Francis Howgill, "The Inheritance of Jacob," in *Early Quaker Writings, 1650–1700,* ed. Hugh Barbour and Arthur O. Roberts (Wallingford, PA: Pendle Hill Publications, 2004), 171–72.

19 Douglas Gwyn, *Seekers Found: Atonement in Early Quaker Experience* (Wallingford, PA: Pendle Hill Publications, 2000), 17.

20 Douglas Gwyn, *Seekers Found: Atonement in Early Quaker Experience* (Wallingford, PA: Pendle Hill Publications, 2000), 17.

21 Louise Wilson, *Inner Tenderings* (Richmond, IN: Friends United Press, 1996), 1.

22 Timothy Ashworth and Alex Wildwood, *Rooted in Christianity, Open to New Light* (Birmingham, England: Pronoun Press, 2009), *16.*

23 Deborah Saunders, "Send Me," *Friends Journal* 44 (May 1998): 15.

24 Saunders, "Send Me," 15.

25 Saunders, "Send Me," 15.

26 Saunders, "Send Me," 15.

27 Saunders, "Send Me," 16.

28 Ashworth and Wildwood, *Rooted in Christianity*, 25.

29 Ashworth and Wildwood, *Rooted in Christianity*, 25.

30 Ashworth and Wildwood, *Rooted in Christianity*, 31.

31 Quoted in R. Melvin Keiser and Rosemary Moore, *Knowing the Mystery of Life Within: Selected Writings of Isaac Penington in Their Historical and Theological Context* (London: Quaker Books, 2005), 7.

[32] Quoted in Moore, *The Light in Their Consciences*, 37.

[33] Fox, *Journal*, 7–10.

[34] Fox, *Journal*, 119.

[35] Margaret Fell, "The Testimony of Margaret Fox Concerning her late Husband George Fox, 1690," in *Hidden in Plain Sight: Quaker Women's Writings 1650–1700*, ed. Mary Garman et al. (Wallingford, PA: Pendle Hill Publications, 1996), 235.

[36] Fell, "The Testimony of Margaret Fox," 235.

[37] Louise Wilson, *Inner Tenderings*, 1.

[38] Raúl Choque Mamani, "A Repentant Atheist," in *Spirit Rising: Young Quaker Voices*, ed. Angelina Conti et al. (Philadelphia: Quaker Press, 2010), 224–25.

[39] Choque Mamani, "A Repentant Atheist," 226.

[40] Priscilla Makhino, "Choosing Life," in *Walk Worthy of Your Calling: Quakers and the Traveling Ministry*, ed. Margery Post Abbott and Peggy Senger Parsons (Richmond, IN: Friends United Press, 2004), 22.

[41] Makhino, "Choosing Life," 22.

[42] Makhino, "Choosing Life," 23.

[43] Charlotte Fardelmann, *Sink Down to the Seed*, Pendle Hill Pamphlet #283 (Wallingford, PA: Pendle Hill Publications, 1989), 4.

[44] Charlotte Fardelmann, *Sink Down to the Seed*, Pendle Hill Pamphlet #283 (Wallingford, PA: Pendle Hill Publications, 1989), 11.

[45] Charlotte Fardelmann, *Sink Down to the Seed*, Pendle Hill Pamphlet #283 (Wallingford, PA: Pendle Hill Publications, 1989), 12.

[46] Charlotte Fardelmann, *Sink Down to the Seed*, Pendle Hill Pamphlet #283 (Wallingford, PA: Pendle Hill Publications, 1989), 13.

[47] Stephanie Crumley-Effinger, "Making Room—From 'Small and Full' to Spacious," *Learning and Leading* (blog), Earlham School of Religion, Feb. 27, 2014, accessed January 7, 2016,

http://esrquaker.blogspot.com/2014_02_01_archive.html. This excerpt has been revised, with permission of the author.

48 N. Jean Toomer, "An Interpretation of Friends Worship" (Philadelphia: Committee on Religious Education of Friends General Conference, 1947), 22, accessed Dec. 9, 2015, http://www.gutenberg.org/files/24576/24576-h.htm.

49 Toomer, "An Interpretation of Friends Worship," 22.

50 Toomer, "An Interpretation of Friends Worship," 23.

51 Toomer, "An Interpretation of Friends Worship," 22.

52 Toomer, "An Interpretation of Friends Worship," 24–25.

53 George Fox, "Paper To Friends, And Others, Against The Pomps Of The World. . . .," in *Works of George Fox written on Sundry Occasions,* Vol. 6 (Philadelphia: Marcus T. C. Gould, Isaac Hopper, 1831), 140–42.

54 Isaac Penington, "Letter to Bridget Atley," in Isaac Penington, *The Works of Isaac Penington, a Minister of the Gospel in the Society of Friends: Including His Collected Letters* (Glenside, PA: Quaker Heritage Press, 1994), 2:507.

55 Isaac Penington, "Letter to Bridget Atley," 507.

56 Quoted in Edward Smith, *William Dewsbury,* 30.

57 Fox, *Journal* , 11.

58 Quoted in Douglas Gwyn, *Seekers Found: Atonement in Early Quaker Experience* (Wallingford, PA: Pendle Hill Publications, 2000), 224.

59 Fox, *Journal,* 104.

60 Mary Penington, "Some Account of Circumstances, 221.

61 Quoted in Keiser and Moore, *Knowing the Mystery of Life Within,* 17.

62 Quoted in Keiser and Moore, *Knowing the Mystery of Life Within,* 17.

63 Quoted in Keiser and Moore, *Knowing the Mystery of Life Within,* 17.

64 Quoted in Keiser and Moore, *Knowing the Mystery of Life Within,* 17.

65 Thomas Ellwood, "Now Was All My Former Life Ripped Up," in *The Quaker Reader,* ed. Jessamyn West (Wallingford, PA: Pendle Hill Publications, 1962), 148–49.

66 Ellwood, "My Former Life," 154.

67 Fell, "The Testimony of Margaret Fox," 237.

68 Edward Smith, *William Dewsbury,* 278.

69 Quoted in Geoffrey F. Nuttall, *Studies in Christian Enthusiasm,* Pendle Hill Pamphlet#41 (Wallingford, PA: Pendle Hill Publications, 1948), 42.

70 Ellwood, "My Former Life," 154.

71 Margaret Hope Bacon, *Love Is the Hardest Lesson: A Memoir* (Wallingford, PA: Pendle Hill Publications, 1999), 18–19.

72 Pink Dandelion, *Confident Quakerism*, Pendle Hill Pamphlet #410 (Wallingford, PA: Pendle Hill Publications, 2010), 6.

73 Wilson, *Inner Tenderings,* 25.

74 Peggy Senger Parsons, *So There I Was . . . .* (Salem, OR: Parsons, 2009), 65–66.

75 Choque Mamani, "A Repentant Atheist," 227.

76 Wilmer A. Cooper, *Growing up Plain: The Journey of a Public Friend* (Richmond, IN: Friends United Press, 1999), 74.

77 Cooper, *Growing up Plain*, 73.

78 Sandra Cronk, *A Lasting Gift: The Journal and Selected Writings of Sandra L. Cronk* (Philadelphia: Quaker Press of Friends General Conference, 2009), 8.

79 Helene Pollock, "Joy: Still a Gift of the Spirit," talk for Illinois Yearly Meeting Annual Sessions, McNabb, Illinois, June 19, 2013, 5–6, accessed December 9, 2015, http://www.ilym.org/drupal/sites/default/files/files/Publications/Yearly MeetingTalks/2013_Helene_Pollock.pdf,

80 Saunders, "Send Me," 16.

[81] Elizabeth K. Gordon, *Walk with Us* (Roselle, NJ: Crandall, Dostie & Douglass Books, 2007), 106.

[82] Gordon, *Walk with Us*, 107.

[83] Paul Lacey, *Leading and Being Led*, Pendle Hill Pamphlet #264 (Wallingford, PA: Pendle Hill Publications, 1985), 12.

[84] Paul Lacey, *Leading and Being Led*, Pendle Hill Pamphlet #264 (Wallingford, PA: Pendle Hill Publications, 1985), 12.

[85] Micah Bales, "Occupying Wall Street," *Religion is Easy. Discipleship is Hard* (blog), September 30, 2011, para. 9, accessed December 9, 2015, http://www.micahbales.com/occupying-wall-street/.

[86] Bales, "Occupying Wall Street," para. 10.

[87] Katharine Evans and Sarah Chevers, "This is a short Relation Of some of the Cruel Sufferings, 1662," in *Hidden in Plain Sight: Quaker Women's Writings 1650–1700,* ed. Mary Garman et al. (Wallingford, PA: Pendle Hill Publications, 1996), 197.

[88] Fox, *Journal,* 14–15.

[89] Margaret Fell, "An Epistle of M. Fell to Friends, 1654," in *Hidden in Plain Sight: Quaker Women's Writings 1650–1700,* ed. Mary Garman et al. (Wallingford, PA: Pendle Hill Publications, 1996), 457–59.

[90] Richard Hubberthorne, "The Convincement and Establishment of Richard Hubberthorne," in *Early Quaker Writings, 1650–1700,* ed. Hugh Barbour and Arthur O. Roberts (Wallingford, PA: Pendle Hill Publications, 2004), 157.

[91] Hubberthorne, "Richard Hubberthorne," 158.

[92] Blackborow, "Visit to the Spirit," 10.

[93] Isaac Penington, "Concerning the Substance of our Religion who are called Quakers," in Isaac Penington, *Works of Isaac Penington,* 2:441.

[94] William Smith, *The new creation brought forth, in the holy order of life* (London: Robert Wilson, 1661), 37. Earlham School of Religion Digital Quaker Collection

[95] William Smith, *The new creation,* 47.

96 Howgill, "Inheritance of Jacob," 173.

97 Howgill, "Inheritance of Jacob," 174.

98 Howgill, "Inheritance of Jacob," 174.

99 John Banks, "The Journal of John Banks," in *Early Quaker Writings, 1650–1700,* ed. Hugh Barbour and Arthur O. Roberts (Wallingford, PA: Pendle Hill Publications, 2004), 183–84.

100 Mary Penington, "Some Account of Circumstances," in *Hidden in Plain Sight: Quaker Women's Writings 1650–1700,* ed. Mary Garman et al. (Wallingford, PA: Pendle Hill Publications, 1996), 223.

101 Sandra Cronk, *Dark Night Journey: Inward Re-Patterning toward a Life Centered in God* (Wallingford, PA: Pendle Hill Publications, 1991), 53.

102 Elise Boulding, *One Small Plot of Heaven: Reflections on Family Life by a Quaker Sociologist* (Wallingford, PA: Pendle Hill Publications, 1989), 49.

103 Arthur O. Roberts, *Drawn by the Light: Autobiographical Reflections of Arthur O. Roberts* (Newberg, OR: Barclay Press, 1993) 146.

104 Roberts, *Drawn by the Light*, 99.

105 Roberts, *Drawn by the Light,* 99–100.

106 Roberts, *Drawn by the Light*, 99.

107 Roberts, *Drawn by the Light*, 160–61.

108 Makhino, "Choosing Life," 23.

109 Lee, *Mystics, Me, and Moby* (Indianapolis, IN: Inner Light Press, 2012) 10.

110 Linda Caldwell Lee, *Mystics, Me, and Moby* (Indianapolis, IN: Inner Light Press, 2012), 16–17.

111 Pink Dandelion, *Confident Quakerism*, Pendle Hill Pamphlet #410 (Wallingford, PA: Pendle Hill Publications, 2010), 7.

112 Pink Dandelion, *Confident Quakerism*, Pendle Hill Pamphlet #410 (Wallingford, PA: Pendle Hill Publications, 2010), 8.

[113] Pink Dandelion, *Confident Quakerism*, Pendle Hill Pamphlet #410 (Wallingford, PA: Pendle Hill Publications, 2010), 9.

[114] Parker J. Palmer, *Let Your Life Speak: Listening for the Voice of Vocation* (San Francisco: John Wiley & Sons, 2000), 63–64.

[115] Palmer, *Let Your Life Speak*, 64.

[116] Palmer, *Let Your Life Speak*, 66.

[117] Palmer, *Let Your Life Speak*, 67.

[118] Palmer, *Let Your Life Speak*, 70.

[119] Elise Boulding, *One Small Plot of Heaven: Reflections on Family Life by a Quaker Sociologist* (Wallingford, PA: Pendle Hill Publications, 1989), 57.

[120] Palmer, *Let Your Life Speak*, 91–92.

[121] Sandra Cronk, *Dark Night Journey: Inward Re-Patterning toward a Life Centered in God* (Wallingford, PA: Pendle Hill Publications, 1991), 60.

[122] Quoted in Britain Yearly Meeting, *Quaker Faith and Practice*, 3rd ed. (London: Yearly Meeting of the Religious Society of Friends (Quakers) in Britain, 2005), 19.08.

[123] Hubberthorne, "Richard Hubberthorne," 157.

[124] Banks, "The Journal of John Banks," 184.

[125] Dorothy White, *A Trumpet of the Lord of Hosts, Blown Unto the City of London,* in *Hidden in Plain Sight: Quaker Women's Writings 1650–1700,* ed. Mary Garman et al. (Wallingford, PA: Pendle Hill Publications, 1996), 15.

[126] Quoted in Keiser and Moore, *Knowing the Mystery of Life Within,* 164–65.

[127] The story of John Bowne's journey is told in John Bowne, *The Journal of John Bowne: 1650–1694* (New Orleans, LA: Friends of the Community College Library and Polyanthros, 1975).

[128] Fell, *A Brief Collection of Remarkable Passages and Occurrences Relating to . . . Margaret Fell* (London: J. Sowle, 1710), 57.

129 Quoted in Mack, *Visionary Women: Ecstatic Prophecy in Seventeenth-Century England* (Berkeley: University of California Press, 1992), 209.

130 Quoted in Mack, *Visionary Women*, 209.

131 Evelyn Jadin, "Presence of the Living Christ," in Conti et al., *Spirit Rising*, 100.

132 Hayo Daniella, "God Can Speak to Each of Us," *Friends Journal* 51, no. 11 (Nov. 2005): 7.

133 Daniella, "God Can Speak to Each of Us," 7.

134 Alexa Taylor, "The Speeding Up of My Heart and the Trembling of My Fingertips," in Conti et al., *Spirit Rising*, 287–88.

135 David Mercadante, "The Subtle Power of Meeting for Worship," in Conti et al., *Spirit Rising*, 37–38.

136 Jessica Easter, personal email to author, July 7, 2014.

137 Gladys Kang'ahi, "Practical Discipleship," in Abbott and Parsons, *Walk Worthy of Your Calling*, 3–4.

138 Elizabeth Baltaro, "A Quaker Marriage," in Conti et al., *Spirit Rising*, 259.

139 Baltaro, "A Quaker Marriage," 260.

140 Thomas Gates, *Members One of Another: The Dynamics of Membership in a Quaker Meeting*, Pendle Hill Pamphlet #371 (Wallingford, PA: Pendle Hill Publications, 2004), 8.

141 Marcelle Martin, "Gathered Into Community Today, part 2," *A Whole Heart* (blog), May 10, 2013, para. 8, accessed December 9, 2015, http://awholeheart.com/2013/05/10/gathered-into-community-today-part-2/.

142 Quoted in Martin, "Gathered Into Community Today, part 2," para. 9

143 Chuck Fager, "Friends as a 'Chosen People,'" *Quaker Theology*, accessed December 9, 2015, www.quaker.org/quest/peoplehood-1.htm.

144 Quoted in Jon Watts, ed., "How Quakers Make Decisions (It's Not Just Consensus!)" (video), QuakerSpeak, June 5, 2014, accessed

December 8, 2015, www.quakerspeak. com/quaker-decision-making-consensus.

[145] Quoted in Michael Birkel, ed., *The Mind of Christ: Bill Taber on Meeting for Business*, Pendle Hill Pamphlet #406 (Wallingford, PA: Pendle Hill Publications, 2010), 6.

[146] Quoted in Michael Birkel, ed., *The Mind of Christ: Bill Taber on Meeting for Business*, Pendle Hill Pamphlet #406 (Wallingford, PA: Pendle Hill Publications, 2010), 7.

[147] Quoted in Watts, "How Quakers Make Decisions."

[148] Quoted in Martin, "Gathered Into Community Today, part 2," para. 5.

[149] Quoted in Martin, "Gathered Into Community Today, part 2," para. 6.

[150] Evan Welkin, "Quakerism Is More Than Man and A Motorcycle," in Conti et al., *Spirit Rising*, 93.

[151] Welkin, "Quakerism Is More," 93.

[152] Welkin, "Quakerism Is More," 94.

[153] Welkin, "Quakerism Is More," 94–95.

[154] Parsons, *So There I Was . . .*, 221.

[155] Thomas Gates, *Members One of Another: The Dynamics of Membership in a Quaker Meeting*, Pendle Hill Pamphlet #371 (Wallingford, PA: Pendle Hill Publications, 2004), 14.

[156] Quoted in Besse, *A Collection of the Sufferings*, 2:525.

[157] Barbara Blaugdone, "An Account of the Travels, Sufferings, and Persecutions," in *Hidden in Plain Sight: Quaker Women's Writings 1650–1700*, ed. Mary Garman et al. (Wallingford, PA: Pendle Hill Publications, 1996), 275–76.

[158] Quoted in Mack, *Visionary Women*, 159.

[159] Stevenson, "Marmaduke Stevenson's paper, of his call to the work and service of the Lord," in *Early Quaker Writings, 1650–1700*, ed. Hugh Barbour and Arthur O. Roberts (Wallingford, PA: Pendle Hill Publications, 2004), 123–24.

160 Thomas Gates, *Members One of Another: The Dynamics of Membership in a Quaker Meeting,* Pendle Hill Pamphlet #371 (Wallingford, PA: Pendle Hill Publications, 2004), 22–23.

161 Quoted in Martin, "Following Leadings Today," *A Whole Heart* (blog), July 5, 2013, para. 12, accessed December 9, 2015, http://awholeheart.com/2013/07/05.

162 Quoted in Martin, "Following Leadings Today," para. 13.

163 Jessica Easter, personal email to author, July 7, 2014.

164 Eileen Bagus, personal email to author, Dec. 13, 2013.

165 Saunders, "Send Me," 17.

166 Saunders, "Send Me," 17.

167 John Fitch, "The Beatitudes," sermon delivered at West Richmond Friends Meeting, Richmond, IN, June 15, 2014, para. 24, accessed December 9, 2015, www.westrichmondfriends.org/6–15–2014.htm.

168 Cathy Walling and Elaine Emily, *Spiritual Accompaniment: An Experience of Two Friends Traveling in the Ministry,* Pendle Hill Pamphlet #428 (Wallingford, PA: Pendle Hill Publications, 2014), 19.

169 Makhino, "Choosing Life," 25.

170 Bayard Rustin, "Letter to His Draft Board," in *Black Fire: African American Quakers on Spirituality and Human Rights,* ed. Harold D. Weaver Jr. et al. (Philadelphia: QuakerPress of Friends General Conference, 2011), 153.

171 Eileen Flanagan, "Africa, Appalachia, and Arrest," *Friends Journal* 59, (June/July 2013): 25.

172 Flanagan, "Africa, Appalachia, and Arrest," 25.

173 Amy Outlaw, "Occupy My Heart, the worship experience at Occupy Philly," *AmyOutlaw.org* (blog), February 7, 2012, paras. 14–16, accessed December 9, 2015, http://www.amyoutlaw. org/2012/02/occupy-my-heart-the-worship-ex.php.

174 Robert W. Hernblad, "A Clerk's Lesson from Occupy," *Friends Journal* 59 (February 1, 2013): 9.

[175] Noah Baker Merrill, "Occupy Together: We Are All Moses," *Acting in Faith* (blog), American Friends Service Committee, October 11, 2011, para. 8, accessed December 9, 2015, http://www.afsc.org/ friends/occupy-together-we-are-all-moses.

[176] Fox, "A Collection of Many," 198.

[177] Isaac Penington, "The Way of Life and Death made manifest, and set before men," in Isaac Penington, *The Works of Isaac Penington, a Minister of the Gospel in the Society of Friends: Including His Collected Letters* (Glenside, PA: Quaker Heritage Press, 1995), 1:85–86.

[178] James Nayler, "Milk for Babes and Meat for Strong Men," in James Nayler, *The Works of James Nayler* (Farmington, ME: Quaker Heritage Press, 2009), 4:159.

[179] Margaret Fell, "A True Testimony From the People of God" (London: Printed for Robert Wilson, 1660), 20.

[180] Fell, "True Testimony," 20.

[181] Mary Penington, "Some Account of Circumstances," 225–26.

[182] Joseph Besse's *A Collection of the Sufferings of the People called Quakers* was published in two volumes in 1753. Other contemporary accounts of the sufferings of early Friends are included in *New-England Judged* by George Bishop, published in 1703.

[183] Quoted in Manners, *Elizabeth Hooton,* 9.

[184] Howgill, "The Inheritance of Jacob," 174–75.

[185] Roberts, *Drawn by the Light,* 148.

[186] Roberts, *Drawn by the Light,* 148.

[187] Roberts, *Drawn by the Light,* 148.

[188] Damaris Mercedes Guardado Lemus, "An Evangelical Friend in Today's World," in Conti et al., *Spirit Rising,* 79.

[189] Kang'ahi, "Practical Discipleship," 5.

[190] Quoted in Martin, "Surrendering Our Selves to God," *A Whole Heart* (blog), July 23, 2013, para. 13, accessed December 9, 2015, http://awholeheart.com/2013/ 07/23.

[191] Makhino, "Choosing Life," 23.

[192] Gerald Hewitson, *Journey into Life: Inheriting the Story of Early Friends,* Swarthmore Lecture 2013, Britain Yearly Meeting, 8–9, accessed December 9, 2015, https://www.woodbrooke.org.uk/data/files/publications/99/Swarthmore-Lecture-2013-text.pdf.

[193] Hewitson, *Journey into Life,* 9.

[194] Nancey C. Murphy and George Francis Ellis, *On the Moral Nature of the Universe: Theology, Cosmology, and Ethics* (Minneapolis: Fortress Press, 1996), 251.

[195] Trish Edwards-Konic, "No Greater Love," *Quaker Life* 42, no. 3 (May/June 2006): 10–11.

[196] Different methods of estimating the death toll result in estimates ranging from around 100,000 to one million Iraqi citizens killed. Hannah Fischer, *Iraq Casualties: U.S. Military Forces and Iraqi Civilians, Police, and Security Forces,* Congressional Research Service Report 7–5700, October 7, 2010, accessed December 9, 2015, www.fas.org/sgp/crs/mideast/R40824.pdf, 8.

[197] Quoted in Edwards-Konic, "No Greater Love," 10.

[198] Parsons, *So There I Was . . .,* 124.

[199] Parsons, *So There I Was . . .,* 125.

[200] Quoted in Martin, "Surrendering Our Selves," para. 21.

[201] Mary Penington, "Some Account of Circumstances," 222.

[202] Quoted in Edward Smith, *William Dewsbury,* 278.

[203] Quoted in Britain Yearly Meeting, *Quaker Faith and Practice,* 19.08.

[204] Banks, "The Journal of John Banks," 184.

[205] Ambrose Rigge, "The Testimony of Ambrose Rigge," in Isaac Penington, *The Works of Isaac Penington,* 1:436.

[206] James Nayler, "Epistle VI. To the Called of God who Believe in the Light to Walk Therein," in *A Collection of Sundry Books, Epistles and Papers Written by James Nayler. . . .* Cincinnati: B. C. Stanton, 1829

(from a 1716 London edition), 686, Earlham School of Religion Digital Quaker Collection.

[207] Marmaduke Stevenson, "Christopher Holder," in *Early Quaker Writings, 1650–1700,* ed. Hugh Barbour and Arthur O. Roberts (Wallingford, PA: Pendle Hill Publications, 2004), 128.

[208] Quoted in Mabel Richmond Brailsford, *Quaker Women, 1650–1690* (London: Duckworth & Co., 1915), 34.

[209] Quoted in Brailsford, *Quaker Women,* 130.

[210] Blaugdone, "An Account of Travels," 276–78.

[211] Quoted in Besse, *Collection of the Sufferings,* 2:204.

[212] William Taber, *Four Doors to Meeting for Worship,* Pendle Hill Pamphlet #306 (Wallingford, PA: Pendle Hill Publications, 1992), 5–6.

[213] William Taber, *Four Doors to Meeting for Worship,* Pendle Hill Pamphlet #306 (Wallingford, PA: Pendle Hill Publications, 1992), 8.

[214] Rob Jones, "Way Opens," in Conti et al., *Spirit Rising,* 69.

[215] Christine Muhlke, "Field Report: Plow Shares," *New York Times Sunday Magazine,* February 28, 2010, 22–23.

[216] Jones, "Way Opens," 69.

[217] Jones, "Way Opens," 70.

[218] Parsons, *So There I Was . . .,* 167.

[219] Richard K. Taylor, *Nonviolent Direct Action as a Spiritual Path,* Pendle Hill Pamphlet #424 (Wallingford, PA: Pendle Hill Publications, 2013), 23.

[220] Thomas Kelly, *Testament of Devotion* (San Francisco: HarperSanFrancisco, 1941), 12.

[221] Makhino, "Choosing Life," 28.

[222] Makhino, "Choosing Life," 28–29.

[223] Quoted in Marcelle Martin, *Invitation to a Deeper Communion,* Pendle Hill Pamphlet #366 (Wallingford, PA: Pendle Hill Publications, 2003), 27.

209

224 Quoted in Marcelle Martin, *Invitation to a Deeper Communion,* Pendle Hill Pamphlet #366 (Wallingford, PA: Pendle Hill Publications, 2003), 28.

225 Pollock, "Joy," 6.

226 Michael Resman, "Self Interest," *Quaker Mystics* (blog), May 11, 2014, para. 16, accessed December 9, 2015, https://quakermystics.wordpress.com/2014/05/11/self-interest/.

227 Resman, "Self Interest," paras. 19–20.

228 Lee, *Mystics, Me, and Moby,* 25–26.

229 Lee, *Mystics, Me, and Moby,* 27.

230 Lee, *Mystics, Me, and Moby,* 27–28.

231 Lee, *Mystics, Me,* 66.

232 Lloyd Lee Wilson, "A Statement of Christian Pacifism," *Friends Journal* 49 (December 2003): 19.

233 Wilson, "A Statement of Christian Pacifism," 19.

234 Eva Hermann, "In Prison, Yet Free" (Philadelphia: Tract Association of Friends, 1984), 4.

235 Hermann, "In Prison, Yet Free," 7–8.

236 Hermann, "In Prison, Yet Free," 5.

237 Hermann, "In Prison, Yet Free," 8–10.

238 Hermann, "In Prison, Yet Free," 11.

239 Hermann, "In Prison, Yet Free," 11.

240 Rebecca Travers, "A Testimony for God's Everlasting Truth," in *Hidden in Plain Sight: Quaker Women's Writings 1650–1700,* ed. Mary Garman et al. (Wallingford, PA: Pendle Hill Publications, 1996), 41.

241 Fox, *Journal,* 367–68.

242 Quoted in Damrosch, *The Sorrows of the Quaker Jesus: James Nayler and the Puritan Crackdown on the Free Spirit* (Cambridge, MA: Harvard University Press, 1996), 101.

243 Isaac Penington, "The Scattered Sheep sought after," in Isaac Penington, *The Works of Isaac Penington*, 1: 127–28.

244 Evans and Chevers, "Cruel Sufferings," 197.

245 Evans and Chevers, "Cruel Sufferings," 97.

246 Quoted in Mack, *Visionary Women*, 136.

247 Robinson, "This Is a Copy of W.R., His Letter to the Lord's People," in *Early Quaker Writings, 1650–1700*, ed. Hugh Barbour and Arthur O. Roberts (Wallingford, PA: Pendle Hill Publications, 2004), 133.

248 *Be perfect, therefore, as your heavenly Father is perfect.*

249 Kelly, *Testament of Devotion*, 71–72.

250 Kelly, *Testament of Devotion*, 73.

251 Quoted in Chad Thralls, "Strained, Breathless, and Hurried," *Friends Journal* 57 (May 1, 2011): 13.

252 Hermann, "In Prison, Yet Free," 8.

253 Kelly, *Testament of Devotion*, 16–18.

254 Hermann, "In Prison, Yet Free," 8.

255 Hermann, "In Prison, Yet Free," 10–11.

256 Martha Dart, *Marjorie Sykes: Quaker Gandhian* (Syracuse, NY: Syracuse University Press, 1993), 102.

257 Quoted in Dart, *Marjorie Sykes: Quaker Gandhian*, 102–3.

258 Quoted in Dart, *Marjorie Sykes: Quaker Gandhian*, 99.

259 Quoted in Dart, *Marjorie Sykes: Quaker Gandhian*, 199.

260 Quoted in Dart, *Marjorie Sykes: Quaker Gandhian*, 112.

261 Quoted in Dart, *Marjorie Sykes: Quaker Gandhian*, 111.

262 Quoted in Dart, *Marjorie Sykes: Quaker Gandhian*, 90.

263 Linda Hibbs, "A Quaker Life in India: Marjorie Sykes," *Friends Journal* 44 (November 1998): 25.

264 Hibbs, "Marjorie Sykes," 112.

265 Michael Birkel, ed., *The Mind of Christ: Bill Taber on Meeting for Business*, Pendle Hill Pamphlet #406 (Wallingford, PA: Pendle Hill Publications, 2010), 3.

Recommended Resources

Books on Contemporary Quaker Spirituality

Birkel, Michael. *Silence and Witness: The Quaker Tradition.* Traditions of Quaker Spirituality Series. Maryknoll, NY: Orbis Books, 2004.

Cooper, Wilmer. *A Living Faith: An Historical and Comparative Study of Quaker Beliefs.* 2nd ed. Richmond, IN: Friends United Press, 2001.

Cronk, Sandra. *Peace Be With You: A Study of the Spiritual Basis of the Friends Peace Testimony.* Philadelphia: Tract Association of Friends, 1984.

Dandelion, Pink. *An Introduction to Quakerism.* Cambridge, UK: Cambridge University Press, 2007.

Dale, Jonathan, et al. *Faith in Action: Quaker Social Testimony.* London: Quaker Books, 2007.

Drayton, Brian. *On Living with a Concern for Gospel Ministry.* Philadelphia: QuakerPress, 2005.

Fardelmann, Charlotte Lyman. *Nudged by the Spirit: Stories of Responding to the Still, Small Voice of God.* Wallingford, PA: Pendle Hill Publications, 2001.

Gwyn, Douglas. *A Sustainable Life: Quaker Faith and Practice in the Renewal of Creation.* Philadelphia: QuakerPress, 2014.

Kelly, Thomas. *A Testament of Devotion.* San Francisco: HarperCollins, 1941.

Loring, Patricia. *Listening Spirituality, Vol. II: Corporate Spiritual Practices among Friends.* Washington Grove, MD: Openings Press, 2003.

Sheeran, Michael J. *Beyond Majority Rule: Voteless Decisions in the Religious Society of Friends.* Philadelphia: Philadelphia Yearly Meeting, 1983.

Books on Historical Quakerism
(in addition to those listed in the bibliography)

Barbour, Hugh. *The Quakers in Puritan England.* Richmond, IN: Friends United Press, 1985.

Brinton, Howard. *Quaker Journals: Varieties of Religious Experience among Friends.* Wallingford, PA: Pendle Hill Publications, 1972.

Davies, Stevie. *Unbridled Spirits: Women of the English Revolution 1640–1660.* London: Women's Press, 1998.

Gwyn, Douglas. *Apocalypse of the Word: The Life and Message of George Fox.* Richmond, IN: Friends United Press, 1986.

Jones, Rufus M. *The Quakers in the American Colonies.* London: MacMillan, 1911.

Trevett, Christine. *Women and Quakerism in the 17th Century.* York, England: Ebor Press, 1995.

Websites

Earlham School of Religion Digital Quaker Collection. www.esr.earlham.edu/dqc/.

Friends World Committee for Consultation, World Office. www.fwcc.world/.

Quaker Heritage Press. www.qhpress.org/.

QuakerSpeak (YouTube channel). www.quakerspeak.com.

Street Corner Society, Quaker Pages and Historical Texts by Quakers. www.strecorsoc.org/.

Pendle Hill Pamphlets (available from Quaker Books at www.QuakerBooks.com)

Abbott, Margery Post. *Quaker Views on Mysticism*, #375 (2004).

Birkel, Michael, ed. *The Mind of Christ: Bill Taber on Meeting for Business*, #406 (2010).

Brinton, Howard. *Guide to Quaker Practice*, #20 (1942).

Coelho, Mary. *Recovering Sacred Presence in a Disenchanted World*, #433 (2015).

Cooper, Wilmer. *The Testimony of Integrity in the Religious Society of Friends*, #296 (1991).

Cronk, Sandra. *Gospel Order: A Quaker Understanding of Faithful Church Community*, #297 (1991).

Dale, Jonathan. *Quaker Social Testimony in Our Personal and Corporate Life*, #360 (2002).

Drayton, Brian. *Getting Rooted*, #390 (2007).

Gates, Thomas. *Members One of Another*, #371 (2004).

Lacey, Paul. *Leading and Being Led*, #264 (1985).

Loring, Patricia. *Spiritual Discernment: The Context and Goal of Clearness Committees*, #305 (1992).

Martin, Marcelle. *Holding One Another in the Light*, #382 (2006).

——. *Invitation to a Deeper Communion*, #366 (2003).

Morley, Barry. *Beyond Consensus: Salvaging Sense of the Meeting*, #307 (1993).

Palmer, Parker J. *A Place Called Community*, #212 (1977).

Punshon, John. *Alternative Christianity*, #245 (1982).

Schenck, Patience A. *Answering the Call to Heal the World*, #383 (2006).

Smith, Steve. *Living in Virtue, Declaring Against War: The Spiritual Roots of the Peace Testimony*, #378 (2005).

——. *A Quaker in the Zendo*, #370 (2004).

Steere, Douglas. *Community and Worship*, #10 (1940).

——. *On Speaking Out of the Silence*, #182 (1972).

Taber, Frances Irene. *Come Aside and Rest Awhile*, #335 (1997).

Taber, William. *Four Doors to Meeting for Worship*, #306 (1992).

Taylor, Richard K. *Nonviolent Direct Action as a Spiritual Path*, #424 (2013).

Wadja, Michael. *Expectant Listening: Finding God's Thread of Guidance*, #388 (2007).

Bibliography

Abbott, Margery Post, and Peggy Senger Parsons, eds. *Walk Worthy of Your Calling: Quakers and the Traveling Ministry*. Richmond, IN: Friends United Press, 2004.

Ashworth, Timothy, and Alex Wildwood. *Rooted in Christianity, Open to New Light: Quaker Spiritual Diversity*. Birmingham, England: Pronoun Press, 2009.

Bacon, Margaret Hope. *Love Is the Hardest Lesson: A Memoir*. Wallingford, PA: Pendle Hill Publications, 1999.

Bales, Micah. "Occupying Wall Street." *Religion is Easy. Discipleship is Hard* (blog). September 30, 2011. Accessed December 9, 2015. http://www.micahbales.com/occupying-wall-street/.

Baltaro, Elizabeth. "A Quaker Marriage." In Conti et al., *Spirit Rising*, 257–60.

Banks, John. "The Journal of John Banks." In Barbour and Roberts, *Early Quaker Writings*, 180–96.

Barbour, Hugh, and Arthur O. Roberts, eds. *Early Quaker Writings, 1650–1700*. Wallingford, PA: Pendle Hill Publications, 2004.

Besse, Joseph. *A Collection of the Sufferings of the People Called Quakers*. . . . Vol. 2. Facsimile of part of the 1753 edition. York, England: Sessions Book Trust, 2001.

Birkel, Michael, ed. *The Mind of Christ: Bill Taber on Meeting for Business*. Pendle Hill Pamphlet #406. Wallingford, PA: Pendle Hill Publications, 2010.

Blackborow, Sarah. *A Visit to the Spirit in Prison* . . . . London: Printed for Thomas Simmons, 1658.

Blaugdone, Barbara. "An Account of the Travels, Sufferings, and Persecutions." In Garman et al., *Hidden in Plain Sight*, 274–84.

Boulding, Elise. *One Small Plot of Heaven: Reflections on Family Life by a Quaker Sociologist*. Wallingford, PA: Pendle Hill Publications, 1989.

Bowne, John. *The Journal of John Bowne: 1650–1694*. New Orleans, LA: Friends of the Community College Library and Polyanthros, 1975.

Brailsford, Mabel Richmond. *Quaker Women, 1650–1690*. London: Duckworth & Co., 1915.

Britain Yearly Meeting. *Quaker Faith and Practice*. 3rd ed. London: Yearly Meeting of the Religious Society of Friends (Quakers) in Britain, 2005.

Cadbury, Henry J., ed. *George Fox's 'Book of Miracles.'* Philadelphia: Friends General Conference, 2000.

Choque Mamani, Raúl. "A Repentant Atheist." In Conti et al., *Spirit Rising*, 224–27.

Conti, Angelina, et al., eds. *Spirit Rising: Young Quaker Voices*. Philadelphia: Quaker Press, 2010.

Cooper, Wilmer A. *Growing Up Plain: The Journey of a Public Friend*. Richmond, IN: Friends United Press, 1999.

Crisp, Stephen. "Journal of the Life of Stephen Crisp." In Barbour and Roberts, *Early Quaker Writings*, 196–208.

Cronk, Sandra. *Dark Night Journey: Inward Re-Patterning toward a Life Centered in God*. Wallingford, PA: Pendle Hill Publications, 1991.

———. *A Lasting Gift: The Journal and Selected Writings of Sandra L. Cronk*. Philadelphia: Quaker Press of Friends General Conference, 2009.

Crumley-Effinger, Stephanie. "Making Room—From 'Small and Full' to Spacious." *Learning and Leading* (blog), Earlham School of Religion. Feb. 27, 2014. Accessed January 7, 2016. http://esrquaker.blogspot.com/2014_02_01_archive.html.

Damrosch, Leo. *The Sorrows of the Quaker Jesus: James Nayler and the Puritan Crackdown on the Free Spirit.* Cambridge, MA: Harvard University Press, 1996.

Dandelion, Ben Pink. *Confident Quakerism.* Pendle Hill Pamphlet #410. Wallingford, PA: Pendle Hill Publications, 2010.

Daniella, Hayo. "God Can Speak to Each of Us." *Friends Journal* 51, no. 11 (November 2005): 7–8.

Dart, Martha. *Marjorie Sykes: Quaker Gandhian.* Syracuse, NY: Syracuse University Press, 1993.

Edwards-Konic, Trish. "No Greater Love." *Quaker Life* 42, no. 3 (May/June 2006): 10–11.

Elam, Jennifer. *Dancing with God through the Storm.* Media, PA: Way Opens Press, 2002.

Ellwood, Thomas. "Now Was All My Former Life Ripped Up." In West, *Quaker Reader,* 144–66.

Evans, Katharine, and Sarah Chevers. "This is a short Relation Of some of the Cruel Sufferings, 1662," In Garman et al., *Hidden in Plain Sight,* 171–203.

Fager, Chuck. "Friends as a 'Chosen People.'" *Quaker Theology*. Accessed December 9, 2015. www.quaker.org/quest/peoplehood-1.htm.

Fardelmann, Charlotte. *Sink Down to the Seed*. Pendle Hill Pamphlet #283. Wallingford, PA: Pendle Hill Publications, 1989.

Fell, Margaret, *A Brief Collection of Remarkable Passages and Occurrences Relating to . . . Margaret Fell*. London: J. Sowle, 1710.

———. "An Epistle of M. Fell to Friends, 1654." In Garman et al., *Hidden in Plain Sight*, 460–61.

———. "A Relation of Margaret Fell, Her Birth, Life, Testimony, and Sufferings." In Garman et al., *Hidden in Plain Sight*, 244–54.

———. "The Testimony of Margaret Fox Concerning her late Husband George Fox, 1690." In Garman et al., *Hidden in Plain Sight*, 234–43.

———. *A True Testimony From the People of God*. London: Printed for Robert Wilson, 1660.

Fischer, Hannah. *Iraq Casualties: U.S. Military Forces and Iraqi Civilians, Police, and Security Forces*. Congressional Research Service Report 7–5700. Posted October 7, 2010. Accessed December 9, 2015. www.fas.org/sgp/crs/mideast/R40824.pdf.

Fitch, John. "The Beatitudes." Sermon delivered at West Richmond Friends Meeting, Richmond, IN, June 15, 2014. Accessed December 9, 2015. www.westrichmondfriends.org/6–15–2014.htm.

Flanagan, Eileen, "Africa, Appalachia, and Arrest." *Friends Journal* 59 (June/July 2013): 22–25.

Fox, George. "A Collection Of Many Select And Christian Epistles, Letters And Testimonies, *Vol. 1.*" In *Works of George Fox written on Sundry Occasions.* Vol. 7. Philadelphia: Marcus T. C. Gould, Isaac Hopper, 1831.

———. *The Journal of George Fox.* Edited by John L. Nickalls. Philadelphia: Religious Society of Friends, 1995.

———. "Paper To Friends, And Others, Against The Pomps Of The World. . . ." In *Works of George Fox written on Sundry Occasions.* Vol. 6. Philadelphia: Marcus T. C. Gould, Isaac Hopper, 1831.

Garman, Mary, et al., eds. *Hidden in Plain Sight: Quaker Women's Writings 1650–1700.* Wallingford, PA: Pendle Hill Publications, 1996.

Gates, Thomas. *Members One of Another: The Dynamics of Membership in a Quaker Meeting.* Pendle Hill Pamphlet #371. Wallingford, PA: Pendle Hill Publications, 2004.

Gordon, Elizabeth K. *Walk with Us.* Roselle, NJ: Crandall, Dostie & Douglass Books, 2007.

Guardado Lemus, Damaris Mercedes. "An Evangelical Friend in Today's World." In Conti et al., *Spirit Rising,* 79–81.

Gwyn, Douglas. *The Covenant Crucified: Quakers and the Rise of Capitalism.* London: Quaker Books, 2006.

———. *Seekers Found: Atonement in Early Quaker Experience.* Wallingford, PA: Pendle Hill Publications, 2000.

Hermann, Eva. "In Prison, Yet Free." Philadelphia: Tract Association of Friends, 1984.

Hernblad, Robert W. "A Clerk's Lesson from Occupy." *Friends Journal* 59 (February 1, 2013): 8–9.

Hewitson, Gerald. *Journey into Life: Inheriting the Story of Early Friends*. Swarthmore Lecture 2013. Britain Yearly Meeting. Accessed December 9, 2015. https://www.woodbrooke.org.uk/data/files/publications/99/Swarthmore-Lecture-2013-text.pdf.

Hibbs, Linda. *"A Quaker Life in India: Marjorie Sykes."* Friends Journal *44 (November 1, 1998): 21–25.*

Howgill, Francis. "The Inheritance of Jacob." In Barbour and Roberts, *Early Quaker Writings*, 167–79.

Hubberthorne, Richard. "The Convincement and Establishment of Richard Hubberthorne." In Barbour and Roberts, *Early Quaker Writings*, 155–60.

Jadin, Evelyn. "Presence of the Living Christ." In Conti et al., *Spirit Rising*, 99–100.

Jones, Rob. "Way Opens." In Conti et al., *Spirit Rising*, 68–70.

Kang'ahi, Gladys. "Practical Discipleship." In Abbott and Parsons, *Walk Worthy of Your Calling*, 3–7.

Keiser, R. Melvin, and Rosemary Moore. *Knowing the Mystery of Life Within: Selected Writings of Isaac Penington in Their Historical and Theological Context*. London: Quaker Books, 2005.

Kelly, Thomas. *A Testament of Devotion*. San Francisco: HarperSanFrancisco, 1941.

Lacey, Paul. *Leading and Being Led*. Pendle Hill Pamphlet #264. Wallingford, PA: Pendle Hill Publications, 1985.

Lee, Linda Caldwell. *Mystics, Me, and Moby*. Indianapolis, IN: Inner Light Press, 2012.

Mack, Phyllis. *Visionary Women: Ecstatic Prophecy in Seventeenth-Century England*. Berkeley: University of California Press, 1992.

Makhino, Priscilla. "Choosing Life." In Abbott and Parsons, *Walk Worthy of Your Calling*, 21–29.

Manners, Emily. *Elizabeth Hooton: The First Quaker Woman Preacher (1600–1672)*. London: Headley Brothers, 1914.

Martin, Marcelle. "Awakening Today." *A Whole Heart* (blog). January 22, 2013. Accessed December 9, 2015. http://awholeheart.com/ 2013/01/22/.

———. "Being Gathered into Community." *A Whole Heart* (blog). April 2, 2013. Accessed December 9, 2015. http://awholeheart.com/2013/04/02/being-gathered-into-community/.

———. "Following Leadings Today." *A Whole Heart* (blog). July 5, 2013. Accessed December 9, 2015. http://awholeheart.com/2013/07/05.

———. "Gathered into Community Today, Part 2." May 10, 2013. *A Whole Heart* (blog). Accessed December 9, 2015. http://awholeheart.com/2013/05/10/gathered-into-community-today-part-2/.

———. *Invitation to a Deeper Communion*. Pendle Hill Pamphlet #366. Wallingford, PA: Pendle Hill Publications, 2003.

———. "Surrendering Our Selves to God." *A Whole Heart* (blog). July 23, 2013. Accessed December 9, 2015. http://awholeheart.com/2013/ 07/23.

Mercadante, David, "The Subtle Power of Meeting for Worship." In Conti et al., *Spirit Rising*, 37–38.

Merrill, Noah Baker. "Occupy Together: We Are All Moses." *Acting in Faith* (blog), American Friends Service Committee. October 11, 2011. Accessed December 9, 2015. http://www.afsc.org/friends/occupy-together-we-are-all-moses.

Moore, Rosemary. *The Light in Their Consciences: Early Quakers in Britain; 1646–1666*. University Park: Pennsylvania State University Press, 2000.

Muhlke, Christine. "Field Report: Plow Shares," *New York Times Sunday Magazine*, February 28, 2010, 22–23.

Murphy, Nancey C., and George Francis Rayner Ellis. *On the Moral Nature of the Universe: Theology, Cosmology, and Ethics*. Minneapolis: Fortress Press, 1996.

Nayler, James. "Epistle VI. To the Called of God who Believe in the Light to Walk Therein." In *A Collection of Sundry Books, Epistles and Papers Written by James Nayler*. . . . Cincinnati: B. C. Stanton, 1829 (from a 1716 London edition). Earlham School of Religion Digital Quaker Collection.

———. "Milk for Babes and Meat for Strong Men." In *The Works of James Nayler*. Vol. 4, 135–66. Farmington, ME: Quaker Heritage Press, 2009.

Nuttall, Geoffrey F. *Studies in Christian Enthusiasm*. Pendle Hill Pamphlet #41. Wallingford, PA: Pendle Hill Publications, 1948.

Outlaw, Amy. "Occupy My Heart, the Worship Experience at Occupy Philly." *AmyOutlaw.org* (blog). February 7, 2012. Accessed December 9, 2015. http://www.amyoutlaw.org/2012/02/occupy-my-heart-the-worship-ex.php.

Palmer, Parker J. *Let Your Life Speak: Listening for the Voice of Vocation*. San Francisco: John Wiley & Sons, 2000.

Parsons, Peggy Senger. *So There I Was . . . .* Salem, OR: Parsons, 2009.

Penington, Isaac. "Concerning the Substance of our Religion who are called Quakers." In Isaac Penington, *The Works of Isaac Penington*, Vol. 2, 441–45.

———. "Letter to Bridget Atley." In Isaac Penington, *The Works of Isaac Penington*, Vol. 2, 507.

———. "The Scattered Sheep sought after." In Isaac Penington, *The Works of Isaac Penington*, Vol. 1, 101–33.

———. "The Way of Life and Death made manifest, and set before men." In Isaac Penington, *The Works of Isaac Penington*, Vol. 1, 14–100.

———. *The Works of Isaac Penington, a Minister of the Gospel in the Society of Friends: Including His Collected Letters*. Vols. 1–2. Glenside, PA: Quaker Heritage Press, 1994–1995.

Penington, Mary. "Some Account of Circumstances in the Life of Mary Penington, 1821." In Garman et al., *Hidden in Plain Sight*, 210–32.

Pollock, Helene. "Joy: Still a Gift of the Spirit." Talk for Illinois Yearly Meeting Annual Sessions, McNabb, Illinois, June 19, 2013. Accessed December 9, 2015. http://www.ilym.org/drupal/sites/default/files/files/Publications/YearlyMeetingTalks/2013_Helene_Pollock.pdf.

Resman, Michael. "Self Interest." *Quaker Mystics* (blog). May 11, 2014. Accessed December 9, 2015. https://quakermystics.wordpress.com/2014/05/11/self-interest/.

Rigge, Ambrose. "The Testimony of Ambrose Rigge." In Isaac Penington, *The Works of Isaac Penington*, Vol. 1, 436.

Roberts, Arthur O. *Drawn by the Light: Autobiographical Reflections of Arthur O. Roberts*. Newberg, OR: Barclay Press, 1993.

Robinson, William. "This is a Copy of W.R., His Letter to the Lord's People." In Barbour and Roberts, *Early Quaker Writings*, 133.

Rustin, Bayard. "Letter to His Draft Board." In Weaver et al., *Black Fire*, 153–54.

Saunders, Deborah. "Send Me." *Friends Journal* 44 (May 1998): 15–17.

Smith, Edward. *William Dewsbury c1621–1688: One of the first Valiant Sixty Quakers*. York, England: Sessions Book Trust, 1997. Facsimile of 1836 book, London: Darton and Harvey.

Smith, Steve. *A Quaker in the Zendo*. Pendle Hill Pamphlet #370. Wallingford, PA: Pendle Hill Publications, 2004.

Smith, William. *The new creation brought forth, in the holy order of life*. London: Robert Wilson, 1661. Earlham School of Religion Digital Quaker Collection.

Spencer, Carole Dale. *Holiness: The Soul of Quakerism*. Colorado Springs, CO: Paternoster, 2007.

Stevenson, Marmaduke. "Christopher Holder." In Barbour and Roberts, *Early Quaker Writings*, 128.

——. "Marmaduke Stevenson's paper of his call to the work and service of the Lord." In Barbour and Roberts, *Early Quaker Writings*, 123–24.

Taber, William. *Four Doors to Meeting for Worship*. Pendle Hill Pamphlet #306. Wallingford, PA: Pendle Hill Publications, 1992.

Taylor, Alexa. "The Speeding Up of My Heart and the Trembling of My Fingertips." In Conti et al., *Spirit Rising*, 287–88.

Taylor, Richard K. *Nonviolent Direct Action as a Spiritual Path*. Pendle Hill Pamphlet #424. Wallingford, PA: Pendle Hill Publications, 2013.

Thralls, Chad. " Strained, Breathless, and Hurried: Learning from the Life of Thomas R. Kelly." *Friends Journal* 57 (May 1, 2011): 12–13.

Toomer, N. Jean. "An Interpretation of Friends Worship." Philadelphia: Committee on Religious Education of Friends General Conference, 1947. Accessed Dec. 9, 2015. http://www.gutenberg.org/files/24576/24576-h.htm.

Travers, Rebecca. "A Testimony for God's Everlasting Truth." In Garman et al., *Hidden in Plain Sight*, 315–38.

Vokins, Joan. "God's Mighty Power Magnified." In Garman et al., *Hidden in Plain Sight*, 255–73.

Walling, Cathy, and Elaine Emily. *Spiritual Accompaniment: An Experience of Two Friends Traveling in the Ministry*. Pendle Hill Pamphlet #428. Wallingford, PA: Pendle Hill Publications, 2014.

Watts, Jon, ed. "How Quakers Make Decisions (It's Not Just Consensus!)" (video). QuakerSpeak. June 5, 2014. Accessed December 8, 2015. www.quakerspeak.com/quaker-decision-making-consensus.

Weaver, Harold D. Jr., et al., eds. *Black Fire: African American Quakers on Spirituality and Human Rights*.

Philadelphia: QuakerPress of Friends General Conference, 2011.

Welkin, Evan. "Quakerism Is More Than Man and A Motorcycle." In Conti et al., *Spirit Rising*, 91–95.

West, Jessamyn, ed. *The Quaker Reader*. Wallingford, PA: Pendle Hill Publications, 1962.

White, Dorothy. *A Trumpet of the Lord of Hosts, Blown Unto the City of London*. In Garman et al., *Hidden in Plain Sight*, 137–41.

Wilson, Lloyd Lee. "A Statement of Christian Pacifism." *Friends Journal* 49 (December 2003): 18–19.

Wilson, Louise. *Inner Tenderings*. Richmond, IN: Friends United Press, 1996.

CPSIA information can be obtained at www.ICGtesting.com
Printed in the USA
BVOW08s0226180316

440684BV00001B/1/P